This book is designed
to the writing of Edward Young, outstanding in the eighteenth century, widely read
and admired during his life and for a cen-
ore. Today, despite some interest in
Young is frequently

Twayne's English Authors Series

Sylvia E. Bowman, *Editor*

INDIANA UNIVERSITY

Edward Young

 80

Edward Young

By ISABEL ST. JOHN BLISS

Professor Emeritus

Western College for Women

Twayne Publishers, Inc.   ::   New York

To
Lucy and Ted

Preface

The occasion of the two hundredth anniversary of the death of Edward Young (1683–1765) may well have recalled the once great popularity of his writings; they were widely read, admired, and influential for over one hundred years not only in the English speaking world but also on the Continent in translation. Historically, they are part of our literary heritage; but in later years the author has been too much misrepresented and his writings too much neglected. Probably no writer was ever more unfortunate in his early biographers, some of whom have distorted the later conceptions of him. When Johnson, to save himself the trouble, incorporated Croft's biased, inaccurate "biography" of Young into his great *Lives of the Poets*, he did him lasting harm. During the late eighteenth and much of the nineteenth century the tendency to read the *Night Thoughts* as practically literal autobiography introduced more confusion. From the erroneous biographical sketches introducing various editions of some of his writings, warped conceptions of the man himself developed which in turn affected the attitude to his writing. Moreover, his works have been badly traduced by the comments of those who seem not to have read them. A kind of traditional denigration has all too often prejudiced critical comments in brief articles in reference books and even in some outstanding histories of English literature.

The last complete collection of Young's works was published in 1854. The only thorough study of his life and works is that made by Walter Thomas and published in French in 1901; and, although this study remains indispensable, new material has since come to light. Since Thomas' work has not been translated, it is not easily accessible. In 1914 Henry Shelley made use of many of Young's letters to the Duchess of Portland, but since that date, too, more material has become available. But many of the old myths linger on. A number of valuable scholarly articles dealing with special aspects of Young's writing and life have appeared in the twentieth century. A brief study of the whole subject should be of value, therefore, in presenting a more valid understanding of Young and his writing than has been available.

When the image of the writer, distorted by prejudiced and inaccurate accounts, has come between the reader and the writing, it is important to correct the image by accurate biographical information and the revelation of his character and personality afforded in his letters and those of his contemporaries. When features of his writing arising from the conventions and circumstances of the period in which he lived are misunderstood and condemned in such a way as to stand in the way of reading, it is important to understand what these conventions and circumstances were.

My aim in this book is, therefore, to consider as truly and as fairly as possible the achievement of Young as a man of letters: to correct the image of Young as a man by seeing him through his own letters and those of people who knew him, and through the events of his life, in relation to the social and political customs and circumstances as they affected him, and the opportunities open to men of his abilities; to gain a more accurate idea of his whole literary career by seeing what he actually wrote in relation to the ideas and the literary conventions of his time; and to clear up some of the misconceptions concerning him and his writings.

Because much misinterpretation has arisen from confusion in chronology in the rapidly changing situations in his lifetime, I have considered the events of his life and his writings in chronological order, as far as possible, interweaving biographical and historical material as needed to provide background material essential to the discussion. As Young's writing is very extensive, a close, detailed, verbal analysis is not appropriate. As much of his writing is not readily accessible, in order to give in limited space as definite an idea as possible of what he actually wrote, I have in the discussion of each piece of writing given a brief overview of the contents and ideas to indicate the purpose, theme, method of presentation; the occasion; and the contemporary setting—literary, political, social—affecting the writing. As the tone and flavor of poetry is best seen in the lines themselves, illustrative quotations are used and Young's own words are incorporated when possible to give further feeling of his method of expression. Emphasis is, of course, on his major writing, and separate chapters are devoted to the *Satires* and to the *Night Thoughts*. A study of Young's life and writing in relation to the conditions of his time makes possible an appreciation of his achievement in the eighteenth century and a realization that some of his writing has much of interest to offer a later time.

ISABEL ST. JOHN BLISS

Western College for Women
Oxford, Ohio

Contents

Chronology

1683   Edward Young born, son of Edward Young, rector of Upham; baptized, July 3, with Princess Anne as godmother.

1695   Admitted to Winchester College as scholar.

1702   Father Dean of Salisbury Cathedral. Entered New College, Oxford, as commoner.

1703   Transferred to Corpus Christi College.

1705   Father died. Young left Oxford.

1708   Granted law fellowship at All Souls College. Returned to Oxford.

1713   First poem, *An Epistle to Lord Lansdowne*. Several essays in *Guardian*. Verse in praise of *Cato* printed in edition of the play.

1714   B.C.L. degree from Oxford. *The Last Day*, a poem, dedicated to Queen Anne. *The Force of Religion: or Vanquish'd Love*. *On the Death of Queen Anne and the Accession of King George*, dedicated to Addison. Death of mother.

1715   As a friend of Pope and Tickell, interested in controversy over Homer.

1716   Gave Latin oration at laying of cornerstone of the Codrington Library.

1717   Tutored Philip Wharton in Latin for six weeks at Winchenden. Accompanied him to Ireland. Met Swift.

1719   *Busiris* produced at Drury Lane, March 7; very successful. Granted annuity by Wharton; received D.C.L. degree from Oxford. *Letter to Mr. Tickell*, a poem in memory of Addison. *Paraphrase of Part of the Book of Job*, a poem.

1721   *The Revenge*, produced at Drury Lane, April 18; printed edition dedicated to Wharton. Young acted as Bursar of Laws at Oxford.

1722   Defeated as Wharton's candidate at Cirencester election. Annuity in arrears.

1724   Production of *The Brothers* postponed. Letters to Tickell, in Ireland, concerning ecclesiastical appointments there. Took orders in the Church.

1725   *Satires I, II, III, IV.* Winter of 1725/26 Wharton left England, bankrupt; became openly a Jacobite.

1726   Withdrew *The Brothers* from rehearsal. Granted royal pension. *The Instalment,* poem celebrating Walpole as Knight of the Order of the Garter. *Satire the Last* (in later collected edition *Satire VII*). Became a chaplain to the Princess of Wales.

1727   "Cynthio," a poem. *Satire V.* Preached before King George II and Queen Caroline.

1728   *Satire VI.* Sermon expanded into a treatise, "A Vindication of Providence; or A True Estimate of Human Life," dedicated to Queen Caroline. *Love of Fame: The Universal Passion,* collected edition of *Satires I–VII; Ocean. An Ode,* a poem to the King, accompanied by "Discourse on Lyric." Became a royal chaplain.

1729   Preached before members of House of Commons. Sermon, "An Apology for Princes."

1730   *Imperium Pelagi, A Naval Lyrick. Two Epistles to Mr. Pope concerning the Authors of the Age.* Became rector of Welwyn, a benefice in the gift of All Souls College. Presented claims on Wharton estate.

1731   Married Lady Elizabeth Lee, widow with three children.

1732   Son born, named for Frederick, Prince of Wales, his godfather.

1733   *A Sea-Piece. In Two Odes,* dedicated to Voltaire.

1734   *The Foreign Address, or the Best Argument for Peace.*

1735   Elizabeth Lee, Young's stepdaughter, married Henry Temple.

1736   Elizabeth Lee Temple, en route to Nice for her health, died at Lyons and was buried in Swiss cemetery. Young and Lady Betty spent winter in Nice because of her ill health.

1739   Lady Betty in failing health.

1740   Lady Betty died, January 29. Thomas Tickell died. Correspondence with the Duchess of Portland began. Henry Temple died.

1741   Unauthorized collected edition of Young's works, edited by Curll.

1742   *The Complaint, or Night Thoughts on Life, Death, and Im-mortality.* The Duchess began her efforts for Young's pre-ferment. *Night the Second; Night the Third.*

1743   *Night the Fourth;* Collected edition of *Nights I–IV.* Young's claims on Wharton estate recognized in part by Court of Chancery. *Night the Fifth.*

1744   Charles Henry Lee, Young's stepson, died. *Night the Sixth.* Correspondence with Richardson began. *Night the Sev-enth.*

1745   *Night the Eighth.* Duchess of Portland renewed efforts for Young's preferment. *Night the Ninth,* and temporarily at-tached to it, *Reflections on the Public Situation of the King-dom, October, 1745.*

1746   The Duchess's continued efforts.

1747   First hearing of case of Charles Henry Lee's estate.

1748   Caroline Lee married to Captain Haviland and left for Ireland.

1749   Mrs. Hallows became housekeeper at Welwyn. Caroline died in November.

1750   First collected edition of *Night Thoughts I–IX.*

1751   Visit of B. V. Tscharner, who recorded his impressions of Young.

1753   *The Brothers* produced by Garrick at Drury Lane.

1755   *The Centaur Not Fabulous. In Six Letters to a Friend, on the Life in Vogue.*

1756   Joseph Warton dedicated *Essay on Pope,* first part, to Young.

1757   *Collected Works,* corrected by Young, in four volumes. Very ill, went to Bath. Correspondence with Klopstock started.

1758   Sermon, preached before King, and printed with dedica-tion to the King. Offered benefice by Duke and Duchess of Portland.

1759   Spence, in March, had Young check accuracy of his anec-dotes in manuscript. *Conjectures on Original Composition.* John Jones became Young's curate.

1760   Young made his will. Arranged to provide funds for school in Welwyn. Friendship with George Keate began. New homage from Germany.

1761   Appointed Clerk of the Closet to the Princess Dowager of

Wales. Death of Richardson. *Resignation* printed for private circulation.

1762 Death of Duke of Portland. *Resignation* published. Death of Dodington. Another collected edition of his works, corrected by the author.

1763 Eyesight failing.

1765 Young died, April 5. All his papers, except account books, burned according to his directions in his will.

CHAPTER 1

Background and Beginnings: 1683-1714

THE whole period of Edward Young's life (1683–1765) was one of extreme political tensions and revolutionary political changes: from the ill-fated Monmouth rising and the accession of James II in 1685; the Glorious Revolution of 1688; the new regime of William and Mary; the problems of succession and the Jacobite support of the Pretender, backed by France; and the accession of the Hanoverian George I in 1714, plots and counterplots, suspicions of plots, and political rivalry developed bitter animosity between the two political parties. At times the line dividing the Whigs and Tories was not always clear and definite; foresight was less able than hindsight to see pitfalls for the unwary. Loyalty to party was of the utmost importance, but there was danger from too strong an expression of it because parties went in and out of power, and an extreme devotion to the "out" party could be a liability. It was also a period in which social class and family background were of paramount importance, a period in which almost all aspects of life were dominated by the need for influence or patronage of the powerful.

I Family Background and Early Education

Young had many initial advantages in family and background. His father, Edward Young, the son of a gentleman whose family coat of arms suggests good connections, had been born on the eve of the Civil War. A scholar at Winchester during the Commonwealth and a fellow at New College, Oxford, just after the Restoration, he early began a career as an outstanding preacher, served as chaplain to Lord Ossory on his military command in the Lowlands, and became his protégé for a brief period before Ossory's death in 1680. By 1683 he had received the benefice of Upham from New College, and he had become a canon of Salisbury Cathedral. A fellow of nearby Winchester College, he had preached before King Charles II and before the mayor and council of London. He was honored in 1683 by having Princess Anne, later queen, act as godmother to his son Edward at his baptism, an honor perhaps due to the influence of Ann Wharton, the first wife of Thomas Wharton, the future marquis and outstanding Whig leader.[1] In the memorable year of 1685 Edward Young was asked by the Archbishop of Canterbury to preach at the consecration of Bishop Ken.

Politically, 1685 had many threatening elements as the plots against the recognized heir came to a head on the death of Charles II; and with the defeat of the Monmouth rising the unpopular Duke of York became King James II, and confirmed public fears by openly revealing his Roman Catholicism. Young sided with the Seven Bishops imprisoned for opposing the king; and, when the Glorious Revolution of 1688 ended James' reign and made William and Mary king and queen early in 1689, he welcomed the change. Many of his clergy friends remained Non-Jurors. Young became chaplain to William and Mary; and he is said to have acted as secretary to the Archbishop of Canterbury, John Tillotson, a great Latitudinarian bishop and probably the greatest preacher of his time. On the accession of Queen Anne in 1702, additional honors came to Young: he was made Dean of Salisbury Cathedral, and shortly afterward chaplain and Clerk of the Closet to Anne. His career seemed to be getting more and more brilliant as an outstanding Whig divine.

Meanwhile, this success of his father promised much for the young son, whose educational steps followed those of his father. At the age of eleven, the boy had been enrolled on the scholarship list at Winchester; and the next year, 1695, he was admitted as a scholar. Winchester, founded according to tradition by William Wykeham in 1376, preserved many old rules and customs of the remote past, suggesting to a modern view a somber and severe environment for the young. A new building, finished in 1687, bore the well-known Winchester precept, still to be seen in the twentieth century: "Aut disce, aut discede; manet sors tertia, caedi." (Either learn, or leave; there remains a third choice, be beaten.)

The daily routine was somewhat Spartan: the instruction was solid, with special stress on Latin; conversation in English was forbidden, and Latin was required. Edward Young's later reputation for fluent conversational Latin and his familiarity with the great Roman writers gave proof of good instruction and of studious interest and ability on his part; the required construction of impromptu verse in Latin hexameters on given subjects would not be without effect. At Winchester, Young made many friends who remained important to him, especially John Harris, William Harrison, and George Bubb. Lewis Cibber, the younger brother of Colley Cibber, was a contemporary there, as was John Philips. Winchester created binding ties, and Young was drawn also to those who had been there before his time and to those who came later—Christopher Pitt, Joseph Spence, Arthur Onslow, Joseph Warton.

In 1702, in the absence of a vacant fellowship at New College for a Winchester student, Young entered as a commoner. The next year his father arranged to have him transferred to Corpus Christi College, where he thought a fellowship obtainable, as the master of the college was his friend. But, as the master was at heart a Jacobite with little sympathy with Whig clergy, no fellowship was forthcoming; and Young remained as a commoner. He continued to frequent the company of New College men: John Harris and William Harrison were there, and he made another close friend, Thomas Tickell. It must have seemed that Edward Young was laying the foundations for a promising future—the best education available; congenial and able friends. But, perhaps most important, there was in his favor the growing reputation of his father and his influential connections. But all was suddenly changed in 1705 when his father unexpectedly died.

Young was obliged to leave Oxford, doubtless for financial reasons, and to take care of his mother's interests, his father having left no will. Mrs. Young went to Chiddingfold to live with her daughter Anne, whose husband, John Harris, already ordained, had received the benefice there through Dean Young. Little can be traced of Young's life from 1705 to 1708. There may be truth in the tradition that he went at one time to Flanders, where his father had some business connections. Such a visit would explain his later references to the Battle of Ramillies and the implication of having seen a battlefield just after the battle. The story of his having gone to Ireland as secretary to Joseph Addison seems to be based on confusion with another Edward Young.[2]

In 1708 he was awarded a fellowship in the Curriculum of Law at All Souls College by Archbishop Tenison, and his return to Ox-

ford was made possible. It is interesting that Young, whose career
was to be in the Church, was again following his father's example;
for he too had taken his bachelor's degree in law. Evidently this
had some advantages: an arts degree candidate was committed to
ordination; the law degree candidate was under no such commit-
ment but his opportunity to enter the Church was not irrevocably
cut off.

II Oxford

The "properly prescribed and regulated curriculum . . . intended to cover the seven years from matriculation to the M.A.
degree, ordained by the Laudian statutes" [3] had suffered with all
the political strains since the beginning of the Civil War. Among
requirements still remaining were declamations and disputations
as preliminaries to examinations for degrees: the candidates "dis-
puted" the propounded points in public, answered questions, and
defended theses in accordance with the disciplines in which each
was involved.[4] The influence of the Oxford system of organization
in a series of logical propositions, by syllogisms, dilemmas, numbered divisions clearly marked, paradoxical replies, and striking
phrases is to be seen in much of Young's writing, sometimes, of
course, only indirectly.

Fellows at Oxford could hold their fellowships indefinitely if
they remained in residence and did not marry. Archbishop Tenison managed to have the residence requirement discontinued at
All Souls College, but proposals to remove the ban against marriage were opposed. In the words of the acrimonious Thomas
Hearne, a Non-Juror and lifelong bachelor, ". . . this Practice of
Marriage is much to the Prejudice of Colleges, and is a very bad
example to Young Men." [5] Another opponent voiced his fear that,
were marriage permitted, fellowships might become hereditary.
Some fellows secretly married, as had Young's father, and held
their fellowships until they were in a position to reveal their marriage.

Some fellows lived in comfortable idleness; some devoted
themselves to study and meditation; many stayed looking for an
opportunity to find a position of some kind for which their Oxford
education had prepared them. These men were, on the whole, in a
difficult situation: "To be continually waiting and hoping for
'something to turn up' is not a wholesome attitude: and eight-

eenth century Oxford was demoralized by constant looking for 'preferment,' whether by lucky accident or personal favour." [6] Fellowships were valuable especially as stepping stones to positions. While waiting, the fellow might teach or tutor, as, since 1700, the professors had given up all teaching, leaving it to fellow tutors; and Young seems to have been so engaged. It was also possible for fellows, resident at a college, to get leaves of absence to act as tutors to gentlemen's sons, and for other reasons.

Just what Young had in mind for the future when he returned to Oxford as a fellow at All Souls cannot, of course, be stated definitely. With an interest and an ability in writing he might add to his academic life a career as a poet. But, without a patron or family fortune, a career as a writer would be almost impossible; and, without a patron, the idea of some form of political life would be indeed impossible. He might enter the Church. Certainly, in view of his father's career, he could not disregard that possibility. As he was not committed to take orders, he could—and did—postpone that choice; and, furthermore, even in the Church he would be handicapped without a patron. In any case, an Oxford education, friends of the right type, contact with men of affairs—political and literary—would be of great value and satisfaction; and these Oxford and London provided. But Young and all his contemporaries knew well the all-pervading significance and the essential nature of patronage.

III *The Patronage System*

The term patronage covers a wide field: social, political, ecclesiastical, economic, literary. No aspect of life in the post-Restoration and eighteenth century seems to have been free from it. The various fields were not only adjacent but overlapping, for many men of letters were involved in politics; and many noblemen, actively engaged in politics, were ambitious to be men of letters, or at least to share in any glory from poetry by showing appreciation —real or assumed—as encouragers or patrons of the arts.[7] For long, court patronage was primarily sought by men of letters, but politicians after the Revolution of 1688 began to replace the court nobles as desirable patrons. Though new opportunities for writers began to increase with the continued rise of the middle class, the greater opportunities for education, the popularity of the coffee-houses, and the attendant stimulus of the conversational spread of

ideas and the development of journalism, most writers remained,
in varying degrees, dependent on patronage, if only to make
themselves known.

That the system was a recognized and accepted part of life is
illustrated in the career of one of the most admirable men of the
time: the cultivation of the right patrons had much to do with the
successful public career of Joseph Addison. With poems in tribute
to the new establishment in 1689 and in praise of William III, he
identified himself with the new regime. Attracted to him by a
poem of praise, John Dryden recommended him to the Duke of
Ormonde. Through a poem, *The Greatest English Poets,* in which
Addison showed lamentable ignorance of the subject but remarkable political acumen by his praise of Charles Montagu, later
Lord Halifax, and through a poem to Lord Somers, calling him a
"potential immortal poet" and asking directly for his patronage,
he secured as patrons two of the most outstanding political men of
the day and he cultivated the connection by frequent addresses.
With such patrons—and his own great ability—he embarked on a
successful political career, eventually becoming Secretary of State.
His election to Parliament he owed to another powerful Whig patron, Thomas, Marquis of Wharton, to whom he was always devoted and loyal, never, it would seem, holding his reputation for
immorality against him nor feeling it unsuitable for the future Mr.
Spectator to be closely associated with him. This cultivation of
patrons is nothing against Addison; the only unusual aspect was
Addison's great success.[8]

Addison's example does show the advisability of flattering prospective patrons, and of keeping on doing so when once secured,
and of acquiring as many more along the line as possible. The
need for flattery, deference, and often what seems today obsequiousness, reflects discredit, not on an individual poet, but on the
then current situation which the poet could not ignore—and
which he took largely for granted as part of the status quo. The
very language demanded by the social manners in addressing
people of high rank differs so much from that of later eras, when
social ranks are less rigidly divided, that readers may attribute
obsequiousness to what was purely formal and proper. The customary way to attract the notice of a prospective patron was by a
dedication full of praise and compliment, in the accepted exag-

gerated style. Though satirists laughed at it, even they used it in
their own serious dedications. As Aaron Hill commented in a letter to Alexander Pope, "He ought to be very well mounted who is
for leaping over the hedges of custom." [9]

IV *Beginning Careers*

At Oxford, Young and his closest friends seem to have been gay,
witty, and sociable, and interested in poetry. Several of them are
included in the well-known distich: "Alma novem genuit celebres
Rhodycina poetas,/Bubb, Stubb, Cobb, Crab, Trapp, Young,
Cary, Tickell, Evans." Young's serious interest in basic values is
indicated in the traditions of his arguments with Matthew Tindal, an outstanding and extreme Deist at Oxford, against whom
he defended Christianity and with whom he held his own in argument. His ability to fit into the occasion, his likable manners, his
reputation for wit and impromptu verse, and his ability as a writer
soon opened up to him some of the best literary circles in London.
Whether, like Pope, he "lisped in numbers" cannot be known. It
may be that with his friends at Winchester and in the early days
at Oxford he varied his academic exercises in Latin verse with
experiments in English. Certainly Harrison, Tickell, and Young,
while still undergraduates and feeling their way toward future
careers, sought to make themselves known and to gain recognition
by well directed poetry. If they discussed patronage, as they
doubtless did, it was not to question whether the system was good
or bad but to consider who would be a good prospective patron
and what would be the best course to follow.

Shortly after Young's return to Oxford in 1708, his friends were
already beginning their careers. As early as 1709 or 1710, William
Harrison, his closest friend, left for London, having published
some poetry which attracted Addison, who interested Swift so
much in the young man that he got him a position with the diplomatic group working on the negotiations for the Treaty of
Utrecht. George Bubb (later Dodington), a stalwart Whig, being
very well-to-do with further financial expectations, left early to
begin a political career as a member of Parliament from Win-
chelsea, a borough "owned" by his family; and within a few years
he was to serve as envoy extraordinary in Madrid. John Harris
was already launched in his life's work in the Church. Thomas

Tickell was establishing contacts in London, and from 1710 Young too was there often; but they both continued in residence at Oxford.

In London, Young became involved in many of the activities of the town and was received into the literary groups associated with some of the coffeehouses. At Button's Coffee House he came to know Addison, whom he greatly admired and by whom he was much influenced. Tickell had sought in his twentieth year to win a patron through his poem *Oxford,* interesting today mainly for its reference to the little group of Oxford friends; but the nobleman to whom it was dedicated died soon after. In 1712 Tickell addressed a second poem, *Prospect of Peace,* to another prospective patron, who made no reply; but Addison was interested in it and praised it in the *Spectator* (No. 523). Tickell's poem of thanks to Addison was admired by both Addison and Steele. Tickell became a protégé of Addison, and later through him obtained a political position. Young too had his literary ambitions and was doubtless working at various kinds of writing, to judge by his production in the next few years.

V Young's Early Writing, 1712–14

Though Young had been busy writing, his first poem was not published until early in 1713. For an appreciation of his choice of theme for this poem and of the prospective patron to address, the political situation at that time must be kept in mind. The years 1710 to 1713 were years of intense political activity. The Tories, then in power, were trying to bring an end to what they considered the "Whig War" and to discredit the great Whig general, the Duke of Marlborough. The long-drawn-out negotiations and preliminaries leading to the Peace of Utrecht and the anxiety over the royal succession, as Queen Anne's alarming ill health indicated that her reign could not last much longer, were matters of the utmost political concern.

Towards the end of 1712, the Tory leaders, to secure a majority in the House of Lords, prevailed on Anne to create twelve new peers of strong Tory convictions. Among these newly created peers was George Granville, who became Lord Lansdowne. A literary career had given him contemporary renown. Greatly admired for his poetry and successful plays, and highly praised by Edmund Waller, Dryden, Addison, Lord Bolingbroke, and Pope, he might well be supposed to be interested in promising poets and not averse to the tribute of new aspirants to poetry. As poet, dramatist, man of wealth, and newly created peer with increasing status in the political world, he might well have seemed a most promising choice for a poet's address. To be sure, Young was a Whig, as his father before him; but he was not in this poem concerned with party politics. And to Granville he addressed his poem.

VI   Epistle to Lansdowne

In his *Epistle to the Right Hon. George Lord Lansdowne, 1712,* Young had two basic purposes: to establish himself as a promising poet with a poem on a popular subject; and to secure the notice of Lansdowne. His choice of the "epistle" as the general form—a kind of formless form—allowed a loose organization which helped him to solve fairly well problems of order and relation offered by the variety of topics he introduced: the blessings of the hoped-for peace to the country, to religion, to the renewal of commerce; the restoration of the arts; dramatic criticism; praise of Lansdowne; friendship; and sorrow at the death of a friend. Some of the topics grew out of the idea of peace, others from Lansdowne's accomplishments, and others were brought together rather by ingenuity. Many of the topics—peace, poetry, friendship—are of interest in that Young was to be concerned with them throughout his future years. Written in heroic couplets, the poem follows the predominant metrical fashion of the day. A general overview of the development of the poem indicates the nature of the material and the expression.

Beginning with a reminder that, in the great days of Rome, even Augustus had often listened with pleasure to a poet, Young suggests that in a similar way Lansdowne, the "Muse's friend," well known for his "love of arts," may listen to him. He then sketches the present situation: after the long, sorrowful years of war when "Fell discord through her borders fiercely rang'd,/And shook her nations, and her monarchs changed," now at last peace seems to be near for England: "All nature seems to wear a cheerful face,/And thank great Anna for returning peace." The poet draws a rather sanguine picture of the peace that is to be secured —when commerce on the sea will flourish, new churches will be built, and spiritual values will be sought instead of worldly con-

quests, and when no longer will maimed and handicapped sol-
diers be seen in "sad, melancholy numbers in each street." Among
the great blessings of peace will be the restoration of the arts, and
poetry will again flourish in England.

Dramatic poetry then becomes his theme—the form in which
Lansdowne had made his greatest success. Maintaining that English drama can hold its own with that of France, Young proceeds
with an analysis of the differences between the dramatic principles
of the two countries, showing a deep interest and wide reading on
his part. Of all English dramatists, Shakespeare, he says, is the
greatest; but he adds that, were Shakespeare to return, he could
not succeed without a patron. He affirms that he himself hopes for
Lansdowne's interest and encouragement: "The Muses write for
glory, not for gold." Then, making Lansdowne himself the subject, the poet continues with a "theme that's able to exalt my
muse," Lansdowne's virtues and abilities. Young's praise is not
without basis in Lansdowne's private and public life and in his
poetic achievement; and, though perhaps a bit exaggerated, it is
not more so than the praise addressed to him by others. One other
glory Lansdowne has—a deserving nephew, gracious, devoted to
his friends, and of unyielding high principles, whom Young figu-
ratively likens to a beautiful cedar that is responsive to the
breezes, though in its upright state unbowed by the north winds.

The reader at this point must feel that the nephew owes his
appearance here to the need for a transition to a theme more personal to the poet: the loss of a friend, unnamed here, a young man
of promise, whose untimely death had been so sudden that Young
had barely had time to reach him before he died. Lamenting his
own loss, he prays that Lansdowne may be spared such grief and
urges him to add further glory to the year of his ennoblement by
renewing his poetic career. The introduction of the last theme,
apparently the death of his friend Harrison, has greater connection with the rest of the poem than appears on the surface. As the
Treaty of Utrecht, then under negotiation, was the background
occasion, the fact that Harrison, a secretary of the British embassy
at Utrecht, had died when on a visit to England on official business links his death with the major theme.

While there are too many topics for one poem and while various other defects are apparent, the real failure of Young's effort
lay in the choice of hoped-for patron. Within a year and a half, on

the death of Queen Anne, the Whigs returned to power with their triumph in the Hanoverian succession; and many of Anne's ministry, among them Lansdowne, were suspected of Jacobitism. Accused of complicity in a Jacobite uprising, he was imprisoned in the Tower for two years, and after a pardon in 1717 he left England for ten years. Indeed, not only did the poem secure no patronage for Young; but it may well have proved to be a positive political disadvantage. No association, however slight, with a peer accused of Jacobitism could be other than damaging in the Hanoverian regime, even to one of a staunch Whig family.

The poem, however, was of sufficient general interest to reach a second edition the same year of its publication. Richard Steele, more interested in the poem than in Young's choice of patron, praised the *Epistle to Lansdowne* in the *Guardian* on May 9, 1713; and he added a "puff" for Young's next poem, from which he quoted, recommending it to the public. Young did not himself include the *Epistle to Lansdowne* in any collected edition of his works, but it was added in a subsequent volume after his death.

VII The Last Day

In 1713 there was a great celebration at Oxford, "Comitia in Honorem Annae Pacificae," on which occasion a great number of poems were recited, glorifying Queen Anne with unrestrained adulation. Concerning the language considered suitable for such royal praise, a historian of Oxford wrote in 1908: "Our own age, which has discarded the conventions of later Roman poetry, stands aghast at the facility with which graduates dropped into adulatory verse whenever the reigning house stood in need of sympathy or congratulation. . . . The Latin verses are formed on the approved models, and deification is merely normal." [10] The English verses on such occasions used the artificial conventions of the Latin. Doubtless this great outpouring of praise to Queen Anne, primarily on the subject of the Peace of Utrecht, gave Young the idea to share in the felicitations and thereby to make himself better known. That Steele had been able to quote from the poem in manuscript in May, 1713, suggests that Young may not have written it in the first place with the idea of addressing it to Anne and that he had adapted it to that end by the elaborate prose dedication.

When it was published early in 1714, *The Last Day* was accompanied by the dedication, but in subsequent collected editions the Preface was omitted as no longer of interest; in later years it was denounced in terms hardly justified by its contents as a whole. While the praise seems excessive to later readers, it is—in comparison with much of the contemporary adulation—rather restrained. In brief, Young, with a veiled reference to the honor Anne had done him in being his godmother, says that he dedicates a "sacred" poem to her as most appropriate, a poem on the most serious subject, the Final Judgment, justifying the theme as suitable at the time of celebrating the Peace in that religious truths underlie such triumphs and that Anne's interest in the Church shows her realization that fundamental values eclipse those of worldly achievement. The picture of Anne, the queen of a great and victorious country, surrounded by able counselors and military leaders, is one of earthly greatness; but the contemplation of a future life, of a glory yet to come, is greater. He prays that her reign may be as famous for religion as for victory and the abilities of its leaders. The theme of the poem is indicated in the title, and the poet says that his purpose is to remove the fear of death and the last day by contemplating eternal spiritual values. The poem has an epic tone, serious and exalted, sometimes faintly reminiscent of Milton. Divided into three "books," each preceded by a Classical quotation, it introduces or hints at ideas which Young was to explore in later poems: the wonders of nature as evidence of God; the supreme value of intelligence; the potential greatness of man; the great virtue of benevolence. Written in heroic couplets, *The Last Day* shows some of the characteristics which mark his future poetry also: his fondness for contrast; his tendency to overuse exclamations and interrogatives; his pleasure in simile and metaphor; and, above all, his picture of the inspiration of midnight meditation, contemplative, serious, but not gloomy. The general scope and development of the rather long poem may be seen in a brief summary of each of the three books.

Book I announces the theme and invokes divine inspiration:

> The clouds and darkness of my mind dispel;
> To my great subject thou my breast inspire,
> And raise my lab'ring soul with equal fire.

Urging men to view "beauteous Nature's face," and enumerating the beauties afforded by each season, the sea, mountains, forests, rivers, vales and hills, he bids them look up to the skies and see there "How great, how firm, how sacred all appears!" Yet, sooner or later, all must be destroyed, even though humanity takes no thought of such an event. All men, subject to sin in some way, living in a world where all is combat and where dangers never cease, may benefit from contemplating the idea of the Last Day. Yet it seems that non-human creatures obey God's laws more faithfully than do men; and, in stories of the aiding of men by "dire monsters," he sees evidence of their devotion to God. The ever useful story of Jonah (related in considerable and not too happy detail) serves as an illustration of God's power and goodness to man.

In Book II Young sketches briefly and with restraint the resurrection of the dead on the Last Day; among the secure in faith are those who had shown benevolence to mankind by their "pious bounties," among whom he includes with praise the founders of the three Oxford colleges of which he had been a member. Thanks follow to God for His "wond'rous gift of an eternal mind," which may live on after the Last Day to see "new worlds tumbling from his spacious hand." The Last Judgment is pictured in terms of a vast theater, where all men are equal; "Heaven's everlasting Son" appears in triumphant majesty, and an archangel "unfurls the Christian flag." Then follows an extended prayer for forgiveness for the past, for control of his passions and emotions, for love of mankind and benevolence to others, and for understanding to behold the evidence of God in all phases of nature: "O, may my understanding ever read/This glorious volume which Thy wisdom made!"

Book III begins with "the book unfolding" and renewed invocation for inspiration. The guilty are indicated briefly, despairing and lamenting. On the other side of the great theater the just rejoice that this time has come. The poet turns to the picture of the disintegrating world, all familiar places disappearing. Then he urges contemplation of the basic values and the realization of the potentialities of human beings:

> Wander through all the glories of thy mind.
> Of perfect knowledge, see, the dawning light
> Foretells a noon most exquisitely bright!

> . . . Worth which must ripen in a happier clime
> And brighter sun, beyond the bounds of time!

And with this joyous picture of ever increasing knowledge in a future life, the poem ends.

The published poem was well received. Steele, a great admirer of it, praised it in *The Englishman*[11] and included it, along with various verses in praise of it, in his *Poetical Miscellany*. He valued the poem primarily for its moral and religious implications and admired the "many noble Flights" in it. Moreover, he admired the dedication, especially—illustrating how taste changes—the very point which later critics denounced: the picture of the Queen on her continued heavenly ascent. Steele had no misgivings as to the effectiveness of the dedication and found nothing "fulsome" in it. The poem, very successful in its day, contributed to Young's reputation as a poet. The topic was popular: the Earl of Roscommon had written *The Day of Judgment;* John Pomfret, *The Conflagration;* Addison, *The Resurrection;* Aaron Hill, *The Judgment Day;* and there were many more. Some years later, the *Gentleman's Magazine* was to sponsor a poetic contest on the "Four Last Things," the Last Judgment being one of them, and there was no dearth of contestants.

VIII   Cato; Guardian *Essays*

In 1713 the great success of Addison's *Cato*, which began its long run at Drury Lane in April and was performed with unusual success by the same company at Oxford, led many poets and would-be poets to write complimentary verse about the play; Young's were among those later printed in an edition of *Cato*, an indication of Addison's approval of them. Young had not contributed to the *Tatler* or to the *Spectator*, but he apparently collaborated to some extent in Steele's *Guardian*. Some of the numbers devoted to the Lizard family (their general story forming a loose connecting device similar to those in the other periodicals) seem to have been written by Young. The essays devoted to John Lizard, the youngest son, who "had the good fortune and honour to be chosen last election fellow of All-Souls college in Oxford" are probably his. One on sacred poetry, in part at least; one on the description of the war horse in *Job;* and one describing Cibber's visit to Oxford with his company in *Cato* are attributed to him. In these essays Young shows his versatility and command of various styles, his wit, his sense of humor, with satiric touches appropriate to the *Guardian,* as well as his interest in various topics and ideas —human foibles, religion, poetry—which appear in some of his other writings.

During the years 1713 and 1714, judging from the numerous references to Young's poems in Steele's various periodicals (the *Guardian,* the *Englishman,* and the *Lover*), Steele was much interested in him. Young was trying various kinds of writing: an "occasional" poem; a serious poem on a "religious" subject, written with an epic tone and an almost dramatic scene; a brief poem of praise; essays, prose experiments in the general style of Steele's periodical. A comment of Steele's in connection with his praise of *The Last Day* in the *Englishman* of October 29, 1713, is puzzling: "I am glad therefore to understand that Mr. Young . . . has now a Tragedy in the Theatre." It seems to suggest that Young was already working on a play, although his first drama to be staged, *Busiris,* did not appear until 1719. He was evidently busy with a good deal of writing, as well as completing preparations for his public examinations for the bachelor's degree in civil law at All Souls in 1714.

IX The Force of Religion, or Vanquish'd Love

The Force of Religion, or Vanquish'd Love, published in 1714, also in heroic couplets, is an experiment in another type: a narrative poem with a strong dramatic quality, it relates the story of the last days of Lady Jane Grey, the nine-day queen of England, and her refusal to purchase her life by renouncing her Protestant faith. A moving story at any time, it had a particular significance at the moment when it was possible to read in it a warning against the threat of Roman Catholicism from the maneuverings of the Jacobites in the critical days of Queen Anne's imminent death. But, on the surface, the poem presents as its main theme the struggle between earthly love and religious faith. The dramatic quality is heightened by indications of scene settings.

The first of the two "books" shows Lady Jane and her husband Lord Guilford, prisoners of Queen Mary. Lady Jane, grieving only that Guilford may be grieving that she has so soon lost the throne, is taken away by jailers; and Guilford, fearing Mary's vengeance on Lady Jane, recalls their lost happiness and the transitory dream of love and empire. Lady Jane, in a gloomy dungeon, resigns herself to her fate, praying only that her husband and her father be spared. Though winds howl round the dismal prison, she sleeps the sleep of innocence, dreaming that the roles of Mary and herself have been reversed and that she has been merciful. Jailers awaken her with word of her "instant doom," and by way of torture tell her falsely that her father has been beheaded. Guilford enters in despairing mood, and Lady Jane is momentarily overcome in anxiety for him. In Book II, the two are imprisoned in a large hall, hung in black, lighted only by a lamp, "like a dim crescent in a clouded sky," and they see a shining ax on a table just beneath it. Queen Mary sends a priest with the offer to spare the lives of Lady Jane and her husband if they renounce their faith. Guilford and her father plead with her to comply to save them; but she cannot do this. Suddenly a large door opens, revealing the headless bodies of three of her former followers. With faith unshaken, believing that her own death will be enough to satisfy Queen Mary, she goes to her doom with fortitude rather than be false to her religion.

The dramatic nature of the poem is evident, and the "romantic" atmosphere of the elaborately described setting and the extreme emotion intensify the effect. The poem was well received and appeared in two more editions in 1715, the year of Nicholas Rowe's popular drama, *Lady Jane Grey*. Steele praised it in two essays in the *Lover* in March and May, 1714. Years later Johnson commended its "felicitous metaphors," but he felt that Lady Jane was "made too heroic to be pitied." The poem was dedicated to the Countess of Salisbury, the young wife of the fifth Earl of Salisbury, whom Young had probably known at Oxford. Any thought that the Earl was worth cultivating as a prospective patron was speedily disproved by his political inconspicuousness and his early death. The dedication is nothing more than the customary flattery couched in suitable formality to address the young Countess; and, as it was entirely separate from the poem itself, it was omitted in collected editions of his works.

X On the Death of Queen Anne and the Accession of King George

Young's next poem, and the last for several years, dealing as it does with the great national crisis of 1714, needs to be read in the context of that time. The political tension increased through 1714: the Tories, after their success in effecting the Treaty of Utrecht, had taken steps, under the brilliant leadership of Bolingbroke, to increase their own power and to exclude the Whigs as much as possible. But the Tories were split in their attitude to the succession to the throne. The moderate Tory, Robert Harley, Earl of Oxford, had been instrumental in passing the Act of Settlement, which provided for the Hanoverian succession and barred any Roman Catholic from the throne. Many of the extreme Tories, devoted to the Stuarts, leaned toward Jacobitism and the support of the Pretender, James, son of James II, whose claim had the support of France.

Because of Queen Anne's jealousy of her Hanoverian heir and devotion to her half brother (though she supported the Act of Settlement, and, as a devout Anglican, was as opposed to Roman Catholicism as the Whigs themselves), it was politically impossible for the Tory politicians to cultivate the Hanoverian court with an eye to future favor. So, making the most of their favor with Anne, whose life was obviously nearing its end, the extreme Tories endeavored to get rid of the moderate Tories in the government. Harley was forced out of office on July 27, and Bolingbroke and his allies busied themselves in consolidating their position. The Whigs and the Hanoverian heirs collaborated; many of the leaders—including Joseph Addison—visited the Hanoverian court and laid the basis of favor with the prospective king. Given only a few more weeks, Bolingbroke might have succeeded in his Jacobite schemes; but on Sunday, August 1, Anne suddenly died. George I was immediately proclaimed king, and the Hanoverian succession, though not by unanimous acclamation, was effected without incident. In all probability the great majority of the population supported it, Tories as well as Whigs.[12] The Whigs realized that it was the one way to guarantee the system of church and government established by the Glorious Revolution. The Tories were, for the most part, as fearful of a Roman Catholic regime as the Whigs; and they supported the Act of Settlement. There remained, however, frustrated Jacobites at home and abroad who continued to plot the overthrow of the new King and who constituted a source of political anxiety, fear, and danger for years to come.

The political tension of the time was, of course, felt in Oxford as well as in London. The Whigs made a point of speaking out and disassociated themselves politically from the Tories there, whose greater numbers sometimes led to Oxford's being considered predominantly Tory and some of the colleges being suspected of Jacobitism. As a consistent Whig, Edward Young doubtless felt, as others did, constrained to identify himself; and at this critical period he wrote his poem, *On the Death of Queen Anne and the Accession of King George, Inscribed to Joseph Addison, Esq., Secretary to their Excellencies the Lords Justices in the year 1714.* In the dedicatory lines, which are incorporated in the poem, the poet expresses admiration for Addison's public life, especially as Secretary of State in the dark days of Anne's death.

In the first part of the poem he glances back over Queen Anne's reign, years of material prosperity, of war ending in triumph and peace; and to the Queen, as queen, he gives official thanks for the country's accomplishments: the Queen and the good fortune of the nation are the same. A few lines recall the military and the naval victories; the achievement of the union with Scotland; Anne's devotion to the Church, her generosity to the clergy, her building of new churches; her thought for the poor.

> August in native worth and regal state,
> Anna sat arbitress of Europe's fate;
> To distant realms did every accent fly,
> And nations watch'd the motion of her eye.

So was she as the head of a victorious nation conducting negotiations for peace.

Now, as one small human woman, she lies dead: "Silent, no longer awful to be seen,/How small a spot contains the mighty Queen!" And with a characteristic epic simile, indicating the transitory nature of life's honors, Young concludes the first part of the poem. Tears cannot recall the Queen, but her greatness will be a challenge to her successor. And, in full accordance with the traditional call, "The King is dead! Long live the King!" Young turns to welcome the new King: "Welcome, great stranger, to Britannia's throne!/Nor let thy country think thee all her own." Britons look to him to end the Jacobite threat: "Repel the daring youth's presumptuous aim. . . ." George's past achievements in battle, council, and court on the Continent have shown his ability and brought pride to England. The poet voices especially the welcome that Oxford extends to the new King:

> What though thy birth a distant kingdom boast,
> . . . Our strict obedience through the world shall tell,
> That king's a Briton who can govern well.

In this poem of commemoration of Anne and welcome to George, written in heroic couplets, in the style then expected in such poetry, with the formal, elevated tone taken over from late Latin verse for such occasions and with rhetorical devices considered conducive to sublimity, Young was concerned with public, not private, matters. The sincerity of his feeling is not to be questioned, as he voiced enthusiasm for the new King, not for George I personally. George, descended from James I, and the nearest Protestant heir, was cordially disliked by the English as a foreigner who could speak no English and as a man whose private life antagonized them. Young did not speak of him as a private individual nor as a great king of England; he merely expressed hope. George's value to the country was that he was the one legal bar to the Pretender, to the threat of a Roman Catholic regime, and to the power of France.

After the accession of George I, a great and lasting Whig victory, the Tory leaders were dismissed, suspected Jacobites were brought to trial, and at the new election the Whigs secured a good majority in Parliament. Stringent steps were taken to prevent the return to power of the Tories. But during 1715 riots occurred in several places, and several Jacobite risings and attempted invasions from France, one led by the Pretender himself, kept the country in a state of alarm and high political tension. Not until the end of 1716 was the immediate danger to the government over. The threat of Jacobitism remained, however, for years; and efforts continued to maintain a Whig majority in both houses of Parliament to insure the stability of the country.

CHAPTER 2

Promise and Disappointment: 1715-22

DURING the first few years of the Hanoverian regime, Young was at Oxford, working for an advanced degree and writing various works which were soon to be published in rapid succession. During 1714 he suffered two great family bereavements in the death of his sister, the wife of his friend John Harris, and of his mother. His only remaining relatives seem to have been the two Harris children and some cousins in London to whom we find only vague reference. His closest friend was perhaps Thomas Tickell. During 1715 the much discussed controversy began concerning Pope's and Tickell's translations of the *Iliad*. According to Joseph Spence, Pope told him:

Soon after it was generally known that Mr. Tickell was publishing the first book of the *Iliad,* I met Dr. Young in the street, and upon our falling into that subject, the doctor expressed a great deal of surprise at Tickell's having such a translation by him so long. He said, that it was inconceivable to him; and that there must be some mistake in the matter; that he and Tickell were so intimately acquainted at Oxford, that each used to communicate to the other whatever verses they wrote, even to the least things: that Tickell could not have been busied in so long a work there without his knowing of the matter; and that he had never heard a single word of it till this occasion.[1]

Pope took this statement as support of his assumption that Tickell's translation was really largely the work of Addison. Young took no part in the controversy; as an admirer of both Addison and Pope, he must have deplored their quarrel. When the two translations were published, Young acted as Pope's agent in Oxford, seeing that some copies reached their destinations.[2]

In 1716 Young was honored by All Souls College by being chosen to give one of the two Latin orations paying tribute to Colonel Christopher Codrington, a former fellow of the college who had left a large sum of money and a great collection of books for a college library. When, according to custom, Young's Latin oration was printed, he included a dedicatory letter, in English, to the ladies of the Codrington family who had attended the ceremonies. While the expression of appreciation of Codrington's generosity is sincere and serious, the greater part of the letter is devoted to satire of patrons who, unable to read, to understand, to evaluate writings dedicated to them, are in danger of praising things destined to the critic's scorn; gentlemen pretending to a knowledge of Latin but unable to understand much; learned men merely repeating what ancient critics said; critics distrusting anything outside the conventional patterns. The advantages of his dedication to the ladies are, he says with some facetious condescension, that no one will expect them to read it, and that, because of its novelty, "it will sell . . . it will make people stare, it is absurd enough." Recognizing the purely occasional nature of the oration and its total lack of interest for the general public, Young later advised that it be omitted from the first collected edition of his work. The dedication is of interest only as showing a vein of gay satire in Young.

I *Philip, Duke of Wharton*

During the summer of 1717 Young's brief association with Philip Wharton began, doubtless through Addison. As this association has been misrepresented in such a way as to reflect adversely on the poet, it is important to make clear a number of points: since Young was fifteen years older than Wharton and since Philip did not go to Oxford, to picture them as gay undergraduates together is absurd; to blame Young for inability to foresee the future notorious career of the attractive youth is equally absurd. A brief look at Philip's life is of value in understanding this part of Young's life.[3]

Born at the very end of 1698, the only son of Thomas, Marquis of Wharton, and his second wife, Philip had as godparents at his baptism William III, the Duke of Shrewsbury, and the Princess Anne. Thomas Wharton's great ambition for his son was for him to become a great orator and a great "patriot"—a great Whig statesman like Thomas himself. Educated at home, and thereby denied the discipline of the great public schools, Philip grew up without control over his emotions and desires. At sixteen he

shocked his parents by an ill-advised marriage performed by a
"Fleet parson." When six weeks later his father died, Philip succeeded to his titles, and a huge fortune and estate, which further
increased by the death of his mother within the year. Deserting
his unfortunate wife, Philip set off with a Huguenot tutor to study
in Geneva, according to stipulations of his father. Everywhere he
went on the Continent a great fuss was made over him because of
his personal brilliance and charm, and especially because of the
great political reputation of his father. Bored with Geneva, Philip
suddenly went to Avignon to visit the Pretender and was there
given the title of duke, contingent on James' becoming king of
England. At Paris, the English ambassador, whom he visited,
tried to overlook his Jacobite indiscretions: he wanted to secure
Thomas Wharton's son for the government, and it was hoped that
the young Marquis would outgrow his youthful aberrations.

On his return to England, in December, 1716, Wharton repudi-
ated all suggestion of Jacobitism, and proclaimed his devotion to
the Whig government. In preparation for a public career, he felt
the need of perfecting his command of Latin; and, probably at
the suggestion of his father's friend Addison, he enlisted Young's
assistance. The essence of the situation is given in an anecdote
whose accuracy Spence later checked with Young: "At that time
of life when the Duke of Wharton's most vehement ambition was
to shine in the House as an orator, he found he had almost forgotten his Latin, and that it was necessary, with his present views, to
recover it. . . . He therefore desired Dr. Young to go to Winchenden with him; where they did nothing but read Tully, and
talk Latin for six weeks:—at the end of which, the duke talked
Latin like that of Tully. The doctor on some other occasions, as
well as this, called him a truly prodigious genius." [4]

When Wharton crossed to Ireland later in 1717, Young accompanied him and at that time met Jonathan Swift. Testimony to the
admiration of the young Wharton was seen in Ireland in his being
allowed to take his seat in the Irish House of Lords, where he
showed the greatest zeal for the Whig cause, and in England soon
after in his being granted the title of Duke of Wharton, with
praise for the achievements of his father and for the promise of
Philip—though he could not take his seat in the English House of
Lords until he became of age.

Meanwhile, Wharton apparently desired to establish himself as a literary patron. When in 1719, after the successful production of Young's first play, *Busiris*, Wharton settled an annuity on him as an expression of gratitude, friendship, and admiration for his literary success, Young could feel nothing but gratitude. Certainly Wharton must have seemed at the time the most desirable patron the country could afford: a delightful companion, a young nobleman of vast wealth, and a promising political figure. It was inevitable that Young dedicated to him his second play, *The Revenge,* in 1721.

The intervening year, 1720, was memorable for the great financial crash, the "bursting of the South Sea Bubble," which brought loss and ruin to thousands and complex political scandals. Wharton lost a great deal of money, though he still remained wealthy. At the end of 1720 he was warmly welcomed when he took his seat in the House of Lords. Thomas Wharton's ambition seemed to be realized: his son was in the House of Lords, an eloquent and forceful speaker, a strong supporter of the Whig government. During this period of Philip's life, as Pope wrote, "wond'ring Senates hung on all he spoke," and to be his friend was an honor. Before long, however, the government's satisfaction in having secured the allegiance of Thomas Wharton's brilliant son must have begun to fade. He joined the opposition in the Lords; and he became a member, even the president, of a notorious group of young men called "The Hell Fire Club," against which a royal proclamation was issued.

Once in the House of Lords, Wharton began to be ambitious to establish a political following to rival Robert Walpole or, perhaps, the Duke of Newcastle, by securing the elections of friends from boroughs controlled by his family. He urged Young in 1722 to become the Whig candidate for election to the House of Commons in the borough of Cirencester, and he promised to assume all the expenses of the campaign and also to reimburse Young for sacrifices of a tutorial position and another college position. The idea of running for election was an entirely sensible one for Young to act on; far less qualified men had been elected. Unfortunately, he was defeated. Even more unfortunately, Wharton did not redeem the bond he had given Young to cover the expenses, and unfortunately, too, the annuity from Wharton was falling into arrears. From this time on Young's association with Wharton waned rapidly.

Wharton, with his ambition as an election "manager," began "promoting all kinds of Elections, Persons who were supposed to be no Favourites of the court," and lost prestige. In May, 1723, he delivered his most famous speech in defense of Atterbury, then on trial for treachery as a Jacobite. Then he started a periodical, *The True Briton,* devoted to attacking the Whig government. By 1723 he was going rapidly into debt and was beginning to sell one estate after another to pay some of his creditors. In the winter of 1725–26 he left England, bankrupt, and on the Continent his fortunes and reputation continued to deteriorate. He became openly a Jacobite, thereby committing the unforgivable political sin. He went to the court of Spain and lived in continuous drunkenness; and after a few years of deepening degradation he died in 1731 at the age of thirty-two.

Young's association with Wharton, therefore, occurred during the period when he was admired in private and public life and when his future looked most promising. Beginning in 1717, this association had begun to diminish in 1722 and was practically gone by 1723. During these years Young had earned the gratitude of Wharton, and he must have felt that he had gained by his patronage. But the failure of Wharton to fulfill his financial promises must have been very disillusioning. Contrary to some later gossip, Young received no later gifts from Wharton. Mere chronology is sufficient to disprove the story of any such gifts after 1723 and any subsequent year: Wharton had no money to give, even if he had any inclination. Young had no association with the notorious and bankrupt Wharton, an exile from the end of 1725. It is unfortunate that ignorance and confusion in chronology have so often brought unjustifiable ill repute to Young because of his brief association with the early Wharton.

II *Poems of 1719*

The year 1719 was an outstanding year for Young: in March, his first play met with success; later, after the unhappy news of Addison's death, he published his poem in memory of his great and admired friend, *Letter to Mr. Tickell;* and then his *Paraphrase of Part of the Book of Job* appeared. Moreover, he completed work leading to the doctorate. Probably as a result of this degree, he received other honors at Oxford, acting as Dean of Laws in 1720 and as Bursar of Laws in 1721.[5] Young was now among men of renown.

His *Letter to Mr. Tickell: Occasioned by the Death of the Right Hon. Joseph Addison, Esq.*, begins with reference to their long friendship, their admiration for Addison, and their present shared grief at his death. Mostly devoted to a review of Addison's career, the poem pays tribute to his many accomplishments in private life as "the source of learning and the soul of wit," and in public life as an able member of Parliament and statesman, devoted to Britain's welfare and "great Brunswick's cause." "In him (illustrious rivalry!) contend/The statesman, patriot, Christian, and the friend!" Then Young turns to their shared sorrow at their loss and to Tickell's consequent "illustrious task"—as Addison's literary executor—of editing a complete edition of his works. The little poem, in heroic couplets, is sincere in feeling and adequate to the occasion; but it is less significant than Young's preceding poems.

The *Paraphrase of Part of the Book of Job* is much more ambitious and more interesting, and it seems to have been one of Young's favorites. Such paraphrases were somewhat in vogue at the time: among the poems of Anne Wharton published in a volume of Dean Young's sermons (which, of course, would have been known to Young) was a similar paraphrase entitled *Lamentations of Jeremiah;* Addison had paraphrased certain psalms; Pope's *Messiah* was a versified version of Isaiah. As Thomas said, in his *Le Poète Edward Young* (p. 322): "Il faut donc se placer au point de vue du XVIIIe siècle pour peser les mérites de cette paraphrase." (One must take the eighteenth-century point of view to weigh the merits of this paraphrase.)

Whether or not Young had some misgivings as to the reader's understanding what he was trying to do, he affixed some elaborate notes of explanation, pointing out "the uncommon liberties" taken in paraphrasing the Almighty's voice from the whirlwind, which he considered "by much the finest part of the noblest and most ancient poem in the world." He had, he said, omitted, added, and transposed. Significantly, among the additions indicated are entire passages on the mountains, the comet, and the sun; and the enlargements are in the descriptions of many of the animals. Young explained that he had recast the Almighty's speech into the form of questions because of the opinion of Longinus as to their contribution to sublimity: "Interrogation seems indeed the proper style of majesty incensed." He had, he said, endeavored to retain the dramatic quality of the biblical source. Young's poem is of interest in itself and as a forerunner of greater poems to come.

Beginning with a brief sketch of Job's misfortunes after long years of prosperity, Young describes the depths of his misery:

> Then Job contain'd no more, but cursed his fate
> . . . nor fears to crave
> Death, instant death, impatient for the grave.

While Job's friends argue about his attitude, ". . . from the darkness broke/A dreadful voice, and thus th'Almighty spoke; . . ." The rest of the poem—almost the whole of it—consists of the speech in the form of rhetorical questions in which the Almighty makes Job realize his own insignificance and the greatness of God. Where was Job at nature's birth, "When the bright morning stars in concert sung?" "Earth's numerous kingdoms, hast thou view'd them all?/And can thy span of knowledge grasp the ball?"

Many pictures suggest Young's fondness for outdoor nature and various landscapes in different seasons and weather. His picture of the unseen beauties of flowers in remote places may well have influenced Thomas Gray's later lines in his great *Elegy in a Country Churchyard*. Many lines picturing summer rains and winter storms suggest descriptions in James Thomson's later *Seasons*. Young stresses the central importance of reason in human nature and of immortality:

> Who did the soul with her rich powers invest,
> And light up reason in the human breast,
> To shine, with fresh increase of lustre, bright,
> When stars and sun are set in endless night?

The second part of the poem, after Job "with trembling heart and downcast eyes" has confessed his error, takes on greater enthusiasm and force in citing the wonders of the universe, great and small, to evidence the greatness of God. Human insignificance is indicated: "Fond man! the vision of a moment made!/Dream of a dream! and shadow of a shade!" Many lines show Young's pleasure in the imaginative portrayal of animals, birds, and creatures of the sea. His favorite was the "warlike horse," a creature which always called forth his enthusiastic delight. Indeed, on the strength of an extended account of the war horse in one of the *Guardian* essays, its authorship is attributed to Young, a circumstance that may suggest that his concern with the *Paraphrase of Job* dates back to 1713. When the speech of the Almighty ends, Job's reply sums up the point of the whole poem, the evidence of God shown in nature and man's place therein: "Oft have I heard of thine almighty power,/But never saw thee till this dreadful hour. . . . Man is not made to question, but adore."

The poem was well received, and a second edition appeared the same year. It was accompanied by the customary dedication, not integrated into the poem. Though at the moment Young had a patron in Wharton, he followed Addison's example by addressing a man prominent in politics as a possible second patron; but, unlike Addison, he made a poor choice: the Lord Chancellor, the Earl of Macclesfield, was not interested in Young or his poem. Nor could Young foresee that within a few years Macclesfield would be discredited and that his public life would end ignominiously.

III *Young's Dramatic Career*

Young, frequenting London as he did from 1710 on, had ample opportunity to see many plays and to hear much talk of dramatic criticism. His association with Addison, Steele, and others at Button's Coffee House afforded contact with dramatists. Current essays in the *Tatler, Spectator,* and their successors provided criticism of drama in general and of individual plays and performances in particular. In a letter many years later Young recalled seeing the famous Betterton's last performance on the London stage in 1710. Evidence of his interest in drama and his use of dramatic setting and tone is seen readily in his early poetry. With these interests and with his contemporary environment, it is not surprising that he turned to the writing of drama.

For writers at the time drama, whether staged or printed for reading, could be a profitable field. It was indeed very difficult to get a play accepted and produced, as the supply far outran the demand. Naturally only those plays written in accord with the taste and desire of the audience and adapted to the contemporary stage and theater could hope to be accepted. With Young's knowledge of the dramatic conditions, with his friends among the influential wits and among men connected with the world of drama—notably, his good friend Steele, who held the patent at Drury Lane from 1718, and his acquaintance Colley Cibber, whose brother he had known at Winchester and Oxford—it was probable that he had more chance than many others of getting a favorable reading for a play—if he wrote one with the essential qualifications.

Though tragedy was less popular and probably less successful economically than comedy, Young chose to write tragedy in spite of his sense of humor and his reputation for wit. What he had in mind was the type most enjoyed at the time, the so-called Augustan tragedy,[6] a conglomeration of elements inherited from Elizabethan and early seventeenth-century tragedy and tragicomedy, with certain added contributions from Restoration heroic tragedy. Heroic actions, illustrious characters, tyrants, villains, violent passions, overpowering thirst for revenge, moving pathos, plenty of bloodshed (off stage, for the most part), and deaths were all expected; and all were expressed in lines of verse, with or without rhyme.

Like everything else in the early eighteenth century, with its political crises and intense concern for, and interest in, political conflicts, drama was viewed from a political angle; and implications were readily caught or read into plays. The audience tended to identify a tyrant with Louis XIV or France; a hero championing liberty with William III or England. Any appeal to patriotism within the story of the play was interpreted as a reference—direct or indirect—to the glory of England, to liberty as a virtue peculiar to England, and to the Whig cause. Anything that could, by even a great stretch of the imagination, be construed as adverse to the government or as in favor of Jacobitism precluded the licensing of the play by the Lord Chancellor, whose power over the fortunes of the theater was great.[7] These facts an aspiring dramatist also did well to remember.

One characteristic feature of the stage should be kept in mind: rapid changes of scene before the eyes of the audience, without the necessary exit of any actor-character already on the stage, were permitted by the sliding flats with their painted scenery, which could be quickly divided and pushed to the sides or brought together as occasion demanded. This ordinary convention of the stage Young made full use of, especially in his first play, with doubtless good effects then, no matter how strange the device might appear in a later age. The frequent "discoveries," by the sudden opening of the scene, afforded a compromise between the pseudo-Classical demand for "no deaths on stage" and the English taste for violent deeds by permitting a quick sight of results of fatal violence and with little loss of time.

The characteristic style of acting was adapted to the stage and the type of plays, and new dramatists had to adapt their tragedies to a performance characterized by an artificiality in delivery quite distinct from that expected in comedy. A solemn delivery with "rhythmic utterance" and with the voice "elevated to a definite pitch" was accompanied by formal and dignified gestures, all considered essential to tragedy. It has been suggested that "grand opera recited or intoned rather than sung" would probably resemble the performance of an early eighteenth-century tragedy. Not until Garrick's time did the style change to a more "natural" one.[8] The dramatists—Young included—hoping to have their plays succeed in the theater, used a conventional style of diction and expression equally artificial and inflated, which owed much to the old heroic plays. To achieve the "sublimity" of the tragedy, ordinary language was considered inadequate.[9] To express passion, devices long associated with Senecan drama—declamation, forced rhetoric, apostrophe, exclamation—were admired and used. Though there was much critical awareness of the shortcomings of the conventions of tragedy, its acting and its style, and though many incisive and entertaining satires were written,[10] dramatic writers looking for popular acceptance could not—and did not—ignore these recognized conventions. That Edward Young followed many of them is not peculiar to him and merely indicates his awareness of the expectation and desires of the public.

With the established practice of the theater season (from mid-September to the end of May or early June) of a constantly changing program for the six weekly performances and of the playing over several times the old plays in stock and reviving the older ones, with a few new ones, there might be presented from forty to seventy-five different plays at one theater.[11] With slightly over one hundred nights, it is obvious that no long runs were possible. If a new play survived to the third night, that performance became the author's "benefit"; it gave him the proceeds beyond the expenses, and it constituted a success. A sixth performance, not necessarily on a successive night, gave another benefit, and greater success; a ninth performance, giving a third benefit, marked a play as very successful.[12]

With so many plays "in the public domain," not many new plays were produced each year: Young's *Busiris* was one of four in the season of 1718–19. The various steps prior to production took their toll. In the first place, it was difficult even to get a new play read by the manager; and, if he read it, he might immediately reject it. Colley Cibber, actor-manager at Drury Lane, had a reputation for rather harsh rejections on the first reading. If not rejected at once, it was read aloud, usually by the author, at a meeting with the managers. Rejections here too were frequent; indeed, Cibber's comment suggests no eagerness on the part of the managers: ". . . upon such occasions the attendance must be allow'd to be as painfully tedious, as the getting rid of the authors of such plays must be disagreeable and difficult." [13] When the play was accepted, the next step was to make sure that there would be no difficulty with the Lord Chancellor, sometimes an uncertain question. Then—after the parts were written out, the casting done by the manager, and the first rehearsal called—the author traditionally read it aloud to make clear his interpretation. After a rehearsal period of some weeks (during which the actors were playing in the regular daily schedule in several different plays), the play was ready for its first public appearance.

The "first night" performance was a very tense occasion: fateful for the dramatist, difficult for the actors, exciting for the audience, and uncertain for all. Rowdy groups of young men often came to damn a play because they did not like the author or the topic, or because they were antagonistic to an actor, or just for enjoyment. Cibber, from his long experience in the theater, described the discouragement often offered new dramatists: "But the vivacity of our modern criticks is of late grown so riotous, that an unsuccessful author has no more mercy shown him, than a notorious cheat in a pillory; every fool, the lowest member of the mob, becomes a wit, and will have his fling at him. They come now to a new play, like hounds to a carcass, and are all in full cry, sometimes for an hour together, before the curtain rises to throw it amongst them." [14] Often steps were taken ahead of time by friends of the dramatist to secure a favorable or at least a fair hearing: commending notices, known as "puffs," were printed in the newspapers; sometimes a goodly number "of necessary friends to start applause" arranged to buy up most of the tickets and so to dominate the audience—a system known as "packing the house." Steele had "packed the house" for the first night of Addison's *Cato,* and Rowe's friends did as much for him in 1715. Certainly a play had weathered many storms before it made its perilous appearance on its first night. It was no easy matter to get a play that far.

Customarily the play itself was preceded by a prologue written by a friend, indicating the coming attractions, and followed by an epilogue of a witty and usually off-color tone, also written by someone other than the dramatist.

IV   Busiris

On Saturday, March 7, 1719, Young's first play, *Busiris,* had its first performance at the Theatre Royal in Drury Lane, with "new habits" and with an outstanding cast for which he might well be grateful to Colley Cibber. In accordance with the conventions of the day, the play was preceded by a prologue "by a Friend," spoken by Booth, who was to play the part of Myron. A prologue preparing the audience for gratifications to come, it indicated that the play would present something new, in fitting spectacle and lofty lines: instead of a familiar hero of Greece or Rome, "the proudest monarch of the proudest age,/From Egypt comes to tread the British stage." But spectacle and royal scenes, a great tyrant, complex schemes, and violence were not all:

> To touch the soul is our peculiar care;
> By just distress soft pity to impart,
> And mend your nature, while we move your heart.

Historical only in name and otherwise original with Young, the play abounds in references to the great resources of Egypt and to the building of the pyramids through the enforced labor of thousands of the enslaved population. The various intrigues leading to the final catastrophe are quite akin to the sensational developments expected in the current Augustan tragedies. In the opening scenes, against an Egyptian setting, the essential elements in the complex central situation are skillfully presented in an expository dialogue of two minor characters, indicating the unhappy state of Egypt under the oppression of the King, Busiris, a tyrant who disgraces "his shining wonders" by his cruelty and pride, and who has aroused the hatred of conquered countries: "Have we not seen him shake his silver reins/O'er harness'd monarchs to his chariot yok'd?" His cruelty and inhumanity are only too well known: "His horrid altars stream with human blood,/And piety is murder in his hands."

Busiris, attended by obsequious followers, enters in full splendor, and by his haughty orders makes clear the enmity with Persia which will be important in the development of the plot. As the royal retinue leaves, immediately "the scene opens" to "discover" the beautiful heroine, Mandane, "attended by priests and virgins . . . sacrificing at a distance." She "advances," and voices forebodings in a prayer:

> O kindly shine on this important hour!
> This hour determines all my future life,
> And gives it up to misery or joy.

Her feeling of the critical nature of the moment is by no means unfounded.

The scene shifts, "discovering" the hero, Memnon, mourning by the tomb of his father, one of the victims of Busiris. Memnon, who relates to Mandane (who has been included in the shift of scene without her leaving the stage) the evil deeds of Busiris and his equally villainous queen, tells of his own eagerness to avenge his father's death. Their plans to marry secretly that very night to protect Mandane from the unwelcome advances of the King's son, Prince Myron, are overheard by a supposed friend, Pheron, who, frustrated in his own desire for Mandane, resolves to get revenge on Memnon. Memnon's fellow conspirators against Busiris enter, and together they plan a surprise uprising that night with the aid of the Persians. All, including the treacherous Pheron, swear on the tomb of Memnon's father to "fast bind" their "souls to great revenge." Mandane's brother Rameses, in passionate vein, calls on the spirits of Busiris' many dead victims to inflame their hearts. But Pheron, in an aside, vows to destroy Memnon through his knowledge of the planned uprising. By the end of the first act, the motivation and preparations for the revolt against the tyrant and for personal revenge and treachery have been made. Suspense has been achieved.

Act II presents a scene of magnificence in the King's court as Busiris welcomes the return of the Prince and the General, Nicanor, father of Rameses and Mandane, and loyal to Busiris. The King promises his favor to Nicanor's daughter. Announcing that he has heard that "there's treason near us," he boasts, "I'm Busiris still," and threatens all his foes with speedy death. Myron, the young Prince (in whom the expository-minded gentlemen see many excellent qualities along with uncontrollable passions— "Pleasures subdue him quite"), left alone with his evil adviser Auletes, confides his overpowering passion for Mandane; and, when she enters, he vows to make her a princess and marry her. Her coldness to the idea arouses his jealousy of a suspected unknown rival. A series of quickly changing scenes discloses further complication: mutual hatred between the King and the Queen, her vow of revenge, and Pheron's betrayal of the conspirators.

Act III opens with news of a terrible storm which has frightened the superstitious Busiris into ordering an expiatory sacrifice of "ten thousand lives." The Queen, hostile to the King, has freed the conspirators, whom he had imprisoned. Prince Myron, struggling against his desire for Mandane, yields to Nicanor's invitation to stay for her birthday banquet. "The scene opens," disclosing a festively prepared banquet room where Mandane, in rich array, is bemoaning the imprisonment of Memnon. An ironically gay scene, with the drinking of health to Mandane, it is interrupted by a summons to Nicanor to rush to battle against a spreading rebellion. Nicanor urges the Prince to stay to protect Mandane. She, reassured by a message that the freed conspirators are lodged in the room beneath, ready to come at her call, is less afraid of the Prince. But, when he too receives word of the conspirators' whereabouts, he suspects that Mandane is in a plot against him. Auletes counsels: "First enjoy, then murder her"; and he relates his plot to outwit the conspirators. As Myron carries off Mandane, the masked conspirators rush in, too late; and Auletes, also masked and mistaken for one of the band, deceives them into running to the city gate to rescue Mandane. Now she is unprotected in Myron's power, and, as she cries, "Memnon!" all Myron's zest for vengeance is aroused.

Act IV opens with Myron in horror at his crime in raping Mandane, with confusion and alarm throughout the house, with the rushing around of Rameses and his friends in pursuit of the Prince, and with the return of Nicanor and the difficulty of breaking the news to him. "The scene opens" "discovering Mandane," and permitting an anguished conversation of father and daughter. Memnon, entering the house in anticipatory joy, as he has completed arrangements for their marriage, meets Mandane in a passionate scene without dialogue. Nicanor is persuaded to lead his army against Busiris and Myron, and he and the young men pledge themselves to fight for freedom from tyranny.

Act V shows the battlefield, all in the tradition of the Elizabethan stage. Constant "alarums" and individual encounters provide excitement. When Memnon and Myron meet, Myron is killed. Mandane, wandering forth in hopes of revenge, is taken prisoner by the King's forces, as is Memnon when seeking her. They are allowed to talk in private. Desperate, Mandane urges him to kill her with a dagger she has concealed in her dress. When he cannot do so, she seizes the dagger and stabs herself. He stabs himself to join her in death. At this moment a march is sounded, and Nicanor and his friends enter in victory, only to see the dead bodies of Mandane and Memnon. News comes that the guilty Queen has been killed by the angry people. Busiris is brought in, wounded and near death, but with his pride unbroken: "Conquer'd? 'Tis false; I am your master still!" He rejoices at the sight of the dead Memnon; and, boasting that lasting fame will be his, he dies. When a friend of Memnon's speaks the final words, he recognizes the greatness along with the evil of Busiris, and points the moral: "Jove lays the haughtiest monarchs low."

As the dead were borne out, or perhaps as the curtains were closed, Mrs. Oldfield, who had been playing the part of Mandane, stepped forth to speak the characteristic epilogue. Great as she was in tragedy, she was even better in comedy; and no innuendo was lost in speaking the lines which delighted the audience but which seem today far from suitable for the occasion. Characteristic of epilogues at the time, it was designed to end the performance with a contrasting tone of jesting for the delight of the "sparks" and the "cits." It suggests that the author, "a virtuous son of Isis," is oversqueamish as he "counts a bold stroke in Love among the vices" and "wastes an empire for one ravish'd gypsy . . . Such is the prejudice of Education."

Busiris, well received on its first appearance, played for nine nights, gave Young three benefits, and was considered very successful. It was played once in 1722, and at least once in later years. Its success was more immediate than lasting, but Henry Shelley, writing in the early twentieth century, hazarded the opinion that *Busiris,* with proper acting could prove effective on a modern stage.[15] It should offer possibilities to the movie industry —if it were known!

The complicated plot, constant surprises and reversals, adequate if not subtle motivation, violent passions and revenge, lofty language, and much violence on stage and off, belong to the conventional pattern of then-popular tragedy. The unity of time (necessitating a rather *full* day) suggests the neo-Classical influence, but the Elizabethan tradition is well to the fore.

Critics in later years have been content to leave the play unread, to dismiss it as "one of the fustian tragedies," and to imply that Henry Fielding had devoted his *Tragedy of Tragedies; or, The Life and Death of Tom Thumb the Great* to ridiculing it. Actually Fielding, in that delightful satire, made many more jibes at Dryden and Thomson than at *Busiris;* and he also included many other writers in his fun. He was satirizing, not *Busiris* in itself, but the characteristics of the Augustan tragedy illustrated in many tragedies. Unlike the conventional tragedies of the day, however, was the absence of the poetic justice at the end of *Busiris*—with the deaths of the hero and heroine just as the rebels were reaching their triumph—an absence in keeping with Young's theory that poetic justice was not at all essential to a tragedy, an opinion held also by Addison.

V The Revenge

It is not surprising that the success of *Busiris,* followed by Wharton's annuity, encouraged Young to write another drama, *The Revenge,* produced at Drury Lane, April 18, 1722, with a fine cast, "all persons being new dresst." The prologue, written by a friend, promised much. The "soft Virgin," the "generous Hero," a "wife suspected," an "injured friend," and a "traitor-fiend trampling the lovely spoil" of virtue, all sound most encouraging for a moving tragedy of the day. And, with further complication for the emotions, the audience is urged to consider the motivation of the traitor-fiend:

> Yet may his mighty wrongs, his just disdain,
> His bleeding country, his lov'd father slain,
> His martial pride, your admiration raise,
> And crown him with involuntary praise.

The play opens, appropriately enough, during a violent storm at night, with the entrance of Zanga, a Moor, exulting in the storm:

> Rage on, ye winds; burst, clouds, and waters roar!
> You bear a just resemblance of my fortune,
> And suit the gloomy habit of my soul.

To his mistress Isabella he explains, to her astonishment, "I hate Alonzo." She had always thought him devoted to Alonzo, his friend as well as his master. Zanga's extended explanation shows the motivation for Zanga's actions throughout the play: six years before, the Spanish leader, Alonzo, in battle against the Moors, had captured Zanga and killed his royal father. Zanga, enslaved but treated well, "with pious rage, pursu'd revenge," but felt "not dishonor'd by his service" until one day in sudden anger Alonzo "smote me on the cheek." Ever since Zanga has brooded on the insult to him—a slave but a royal Moor—and has sought an occasion "of ample vengeance."

At present Zanga hopes to hurt Alonzo through his military ambition, "dearer to him than his soul," and has betrayed to the Moorish camp Alonzo's plans for a surprise attack. But word comes that Alonzo is returning in triumph, though suspecting some betrayal of his plans. His friend, Don Carlos, recently freed by Alonzo from a long Moorish captivity, eagerly awaits his return and recalls all he owes to Alonzo, including Alonzo's promise to win Leonora for him during his absence. Leonora's father, favoring Carlos for his great wealth, forces her to agree to marry him, though she loves the absent Alonzo. Carlos tries to win her love by telling of his devotion for her which had endured through his captivity and had caused him to rush to her the moment he was freed. Trumpets announce the victorious Alonzo, and the two friends meet with joy, vowing that their friendship surpasses all else in value. When, alone with his trusted Zanga, Alonzo confides his misery at the thought of having wronged Carlos by trying to win Leonora for himself, believing that Carlos had died in captivity,

Zanga's hopes of vengeance begin to revive. Leonora and Alonzo are torn between love for each other and friendship for Carlos.

As Act II opens, events have taken a turn: news that Carlos' fortune has been lost in shipwreck has changed the father's mind; and he now wants Alonzo to marry his daughter. Alonzo, after momentary joy, is concerned over thought of Carlos' distress. Zanga is struck with an idea:

> Ha! it dawns. . . .
> Vengeance is still alive. . . .
> With all her snakes erect upon her crest,
> She stalks in view, and fires me with her charms.

His base plan takes shape—to persuade Alonzo to ask Carlos to consent to the marriage and to persuade Carlos to agree: then, to arouse Alonzo's jealous suspicion as to why Carlos would consent. Pretending deepest friendship to both, Zanga overcomes their hesitation and revels at each successful step: "Look down, O holy prophet! see me torture/This Christian dog, this infidel!"

By Act III, the marriage of Leonora and Alonzo has taken place; and Zanga proceeds with his plot. By a letter purporting to be from Carlos, picked up as intended by Alonzo but dropped unread, and torn up by Zanga, who believes that uncertainty as to its contents will be more disturbing to Alonzo than knowledge, Zanga arouses Alonzo's suspicions, fans them while pretending sympathy, and suggests that it was too bad that Alonzo had sent the liberated Carlos so hastily to court and given some villain basis for the senseless letter. But Alonzo did not send him. "Not send him! Ha!—That strikes me." Why then had Carlos come so hastily? By innuendo, hesitation, simulated surprise, Zanga tortures Alonzo. Then, with pretended encouragement, he reassures his victim:

> Had he enjoy'd her,
> Be most assur'd, he had resign'd her to you
> With less reluctance.

Resigned her? The distracted Alonzo is convinced. Zanga, pretending alarm that the letter might have had some truth in it, bids Alonzo calm himself in the realization that jealousy tends to "swell small things to great." Zanga, left alone, feels some qualms about what he is doing; but he quickly recovers his ardor for revenge.

Act IV is full of suspense. Zanga, dismayed at Alonzo's intention of talking the whole matter over with Leonora, promises to tell him something further about Carlos' midnight return; but, when Leonora comes to urge him to join the wedding guests, the sight of her removes all Alonzo's suspicions and he promises to follow her in a moment. Zanga must start again. With feigned reluctance he tells Alonzo that not only had he seen two lovers in the bower that midnight but had seen Leonora and Carlos emerge. Alonzo, his suspicions now turned to conviction, plans to murder them both. Once again, however, the sight of Leonora revives his faith in her innocence. But Zanga's poisonous suggestions renew the distraught Alonzo's suspicions, and he vows to kill Leonora in the bower on this their bridal day.

Act V opens with Alonzo, repenting with horror the plans made for the murder of his friend Carlos and stunned by Zanga's news that Carlos has already died, blessing his dear friend Alonzo. As Alonzo goes to find Leonora in the bower, Zanga rejoices, in customary vivid imagery:

> Sisters of Acheron, go hence hand in hand; . . .
> May serpents winding up the trees, let fall
> Their hissing necks upon them from above.

In the bower, Alonzo, overcome by the beauty and apparent innocence of the sleeping Leonora and after a conversation which baffles her, drops his dagger and leaves. Zanga, entering to taste the sweetness of revenge, is aghast. To her question as to who could have caused Alonzo's jealousy, he answers ironically: "Some villain; who, hell knows." Alonzo, returning in fury against Zanga, pours out his love to Leonora; but, when she asks why he had been jealous, his suspicions revive. Deeply hurt, she refuses to answer any questions; and Alonzo believes she is hiding her guilt. After a tense passage of short, quick dialogue, she, despairing of convincing him of her innocence, suddenly seizes the dagger and stabs herself. In horror, Alonzo calls for help; and he begins to think he may be wrong. But his cup of bitterness is not yet full. When Zanga, to enjoy the full measure of his revenge, tells him that he had contrived it all and that Alonzo was indeed wrong, Alonzo stabs himself and dies. Zanga watches in satisfaction, though—as was characteristic of the last lines of a tragedy—he admits Alonzo's virtues.

The epilogue, written in the comic strain expected and accepted at the time, was spoken by one of the actresses. Taking the attitude of the contemporary comedies of domestic intrigue, scoffing at all the "to-do" over a mere suspicion of infidelity, it suggests that the big mistake was the unconsummated nature of the marriage. The slightly humorous effect is heightened by the abundance of double rhyme, as well as by the *double-entendre* of the whole.

The reference to the prophecy that the play would live "at least six days of fame" was actually an indication of the likelihood of its success. Though *The Revenge* was less successful immediately than *Busiris,* with six performances and two benefits instead of nine performances and three benefits, and though the copyright for the printed edition brought less than that for Young's first play, it was to become one of the most successful plays of the century, played over and over as one of the stock plays of the company, and holding the stage even into the nineteenth century. The great David Garrick called it the "best modern play." [16] John Doran, in writing of the dramatists of the period of George I, said: "The name of Young alone survives in the memory, and that but for one tragedy, *The Revenge.*" [17] David Baker assigns it "a place in the very front rank of our dramatic writings." [18]

Examination of the play shows that it is a well-planned, effective Augustan tragedy. It has, of course, many echoes of *Othello,* and indeed of other Shakespearean plays. Suspense is well achieved. With few characters and not too many complicating threads in the story, it is much more concentrated in effect than *Busiris.* The motivation, indicated clearly in the prologue and shown at length early in the first scene, is well sustained and adequate. Occasional criticism that Zanga lacked motivation seems to be made from the point of view of the Spaniards. But Zanga, a Moorish prince and an ardent warrior against the hated enemies of his race and kingdom, a slave-servant to the slayer of his father, nursing in secret his desire for vengeance, felt Alonzo's blow to be symbolic of his slavery and a degradation of his royal rank—the final incomprehensible, unbearable insult to his personality. When the opportunity for revenge came, what did it matter to Zanga if Carlos and Leonora also became victims of his plot? To Zanga, his was vengeance not only for a personal wrong, no matter how terrible, but also for his lost kingdom, his frustrated followers, the conquest of all Moors.

Zanga became one of the great dramatic roles, played by outstanding actors. On the first performance of the play, Cibber had felt it necessary to reassure Mr. Mills that, though Mr. Booth was to take the part of Alonzo, Mr. Wilks that of Don Carlos, and Mr. Thurmond that of Don Alvarez, the part of Zanga really had great possibilities and that it was not given to him as a minor or unimportant role. A bit later, Elrington played Zanga: "After Dr. Young had seen Elrington play it, he went round, shook him cordially by the hand, thanked him heartily, and declared he had never seen the part done such justice to." [19] Quin was a famous Zanga, and later Mossop was outstanding in the role while playing in Garrick's company: "Zanga, in the *Revenge,* was his grand performance, and in this, even Quin was not superior to him. . . ." [20]

The printed play was dedicated to the Duke of Wharton. Having received an annuity from him shortly after the production of *Busiris,* how could Young, early in 1722, have dedicated his second play to anyone else? His implication in the dedication that Wharton's suggestions and encouragement had contributed greatly was little more than a polite gesture. His allusions to the young Duke's public virtues and "grace and power of public eloquence" and his promise of even greater glory in his career were but statements of general opinion at the time. The enumeration of his private virtues—"variety of polite and useful studies," his "beautiful mixture of learning and genius," "a mind equally knowing in books and men," his wit in conversation and his sweet disposition—all seemed to be borne out in actuality in early 1722, the date of the dedication. The expression of the gratitude of Oxford for his generous donations and of Young's gratitude to him was certainly deserved and sincere.

In later editions of the play in Young's collected works, the dedication was omitted rather naturally as taking up space, as being of ephemeral interest, and as not being an integral part of the play. To reproach Young for omitting it—or, using a slanted word, "suppressing" it—is unwarranted. To be sure, within less than two years of its writing, much that was said in the dedication was no longer true of the rapidly degenerating Duke of Wharton.

CHAPTER 3

Life's Follies: The Satires, 1725-28

THE decade of the 1720's, one of the most complex and critical in Young's whole career, was also marked by some of his greatest literary accomplishments and by decisions which affected the rest of his life. In 1720 his close friend George Bubb inherited the great estate and fortune of his maternal uncle; and, in accordance with the uncle's stipulation, he legally adopted his name, Dodington. Now in England after his experience in the diplomatic world in Madrid, Dodington had entered on an active political career. He poured vast sums of money into the improvement of his estate at Eastbury and into the building of a great mansion, of which Vanbrugh was the architect. Here he extended hospitality to many outstanding people. Young, a lifelong friend from Winchester and Oxford days, was a welcome and frequent visitor. Dodington, with some poetical aspirations of his own, sought Young's criticism and suggestions.

Young was evidently visiting at Eastbury in 1722, for in that year a mutual friend, Christopher Pitt, sent him a verse letter inviting him to come to see the military review at Sarum Field. The lines give a glimpse of the friendly hospitality Young was enjoying, of wine and wit and tobacco; of watching the building of the mansion; of walking in the shady groves and the celebrated gardens. Pitt evidently believed that Young was writing another play.[1] At Eastbury Young met James Thomson, who became a kind of protégé of Dodington. Young also met Voltaire there, probably in 1726; and in a discussion of *Paradise Lost*, according to one of Spence's anecdotes, Young replied to Voltaire's objection to the allegorical figures of Sin and Death in an impromptu distich: "Thou'rt so ingenious, profligate, and thin,/That thou thyself art Milton's death and sin." [2] Another anecdote of Eastbury seems to come from about the same time: the story in which Young maintained that a night of a terrific storm was a beautiful one—

"The Lord is abroad." Contacts with aristocratic and literary people at Eastbury and in London suggest that Young was in social demand. He was known for his manners, his wit, his conversation.

I *The* Satires

Young's greatest achievement of the decade of the 1720's—and one of the greatest of his whole life—was without question the writing of his *Satires*. In these are reflected his ideas, observations, and values from years of observation of contemporary life, and from his wide reading in Classical satire and that of France and England, especially that of Dryden, Steele, and above all Addison. Young had himself and from his own experience written essays in satirical vein for the *Guardian,* and he had developed his own theory of satire. The actual writing of his *Satires* was the work of several years: in 1724, he sent part of *Satire I* to Tickell for his opinion; in 1725, his first four satires were published separately at intervals; in 1726, the one now numbered VII was published; and in 1727 and 1728, V and VI appeared. Later in 1728 a collected edition appeared, with the title *Love of Fame: The Universal Passion: in Seven Characteristical Satires,* with an extended preface expressing his theory of satire. It is well to look at some of his salient points in his own words:

No man can converse much in the world, but, at what he meets with, he must either be insensible, or grieve, or be angry, or smile. . . . Now to smile at it, and turn it into ridicule, I think most eligible, as it hurts ourselves least, and gives vice and folly the greatest offence; and that for this reason, because what men aim at by them is, generally, public opinion and esteem; which truth is the subject of the following Satires, and joins them together as several branches from the same root; an unity of design which has not, I think, in a set of Satires, been attempted before. . . . Moreover, laughing satire bids the fairest for success. . . . This kind of satire only has any delicacy in it. Of this delicacy Horace is the best master: he appears in good humour while he censures. . . . Juvenal is ever in a passion. . . . There are some prose satirists of the greatest delicacy and wit; the last of which can never, or should never, succeed without the former.

Young's seven satires are, then, laughing satires, new in having an underlying, unifying theme, not personal, but general: "I am not conscious of the least malevolence to any particular person."

Young's "persona" throughout is that of a mature, rather disillusioned, sophisticated man, with a keen observation of the follies and foibles of men and women and a knowledge of a wide range of life, particularly in fashionable circles.

But, besides the new unity of design in the series, originality is indicated also in the term "characteristical." Young was doing for the first time in verse something of what had been done in prose by Addison and Steele: making use of the popular genre of the "character" as a device for satire. Thus Young gave his general satire a personal effect through fictitious, illustrative examples. He was not just imitating the authors of the *Tatler* and the *Spectator;* he brought his own insight, observation, and, above all, expression. Naturally many examples are reminiscent of those used by those two great social satirists, for he was concerned with almost the same period of the human scene. More particularly, his method involves frequently a brief general comment followed by brief sketches of one or several individuals illustrating and developing the folly or vice in question, often in a series of distichs and occasionally in an extended description of one individual; then may come a comment arising from the preceding sketches and leading to a new topic growing out of "the love of fame."

As each satire was published separately and as the whole series was probably not planned ahead, there is, in spite of his "unity of design," no clearly perceptible over-all plan of organization. Though there is some difference of material and emphasis in the individual satires, the structure in all is loose, one folly suggesting another: "My growing subject seems but just begun/And, chariot-like, I kindle as I run." The implied standards by which he measures the follies and vices are those of human relations and decorum, morality, and religion. Human nature he sees as potentially good, but as corrupted by ambition, by greed for wealth and power, and by abandonment to the passions, which in themselves are good or bad only as they are directed. The evils in social relations he most assails are those of hardheartedness, deceit, and exploitation for one's own ends. He is not concerned with a deep analysis of these shortcomings of man but rather with an amused look at the absurdities that they lead to in the pretenses and follies of life. It is only toward the end of the series that he is more concerned with deeper considerations of more serious social vices.

Because of the nature of the satires, it is impossible to summarize the whole series meaningfully. A glance at some of the outstanding topics and characters of the individual satires suggests, however, not only the subject matter but the effective expression.

II   Satire I

Satire I begins by indicating the timeliness and appropriateness of satire, for the age is marked by follies and vices in its every aspect: "The love of praise, howe'er concealed by art,/Reigns more or less, and glows in ev'ry heart." It is found in the proud, the monarch, the scholar, the Whigs, the Tories—in all phases of life, and even in death: "Nor ends with life; but nods in sable plumes,/Adorns our hearse, and flatters on our tombs." And this love of fame incites men to strange things: "Some lords have learn'd to spell. . . ." It leads Globose, pompous and self-important, but with no ideas, to arise to speak in public and to say— nothing: "He hems, and is deliver'd of his mouse." It leads many to talk exclusively of themselves: "It makes dear self on well-bred tongues prevail,/ And *I* the little hero of each tale."

As more and more examples occur to him, Young invokes the aid of Homer to fashion an epic catalogue. The first to come forward is the titled aristocrat whose sole claim to fame is his ancestry: "He stands for fame on his forefather's feet." A newly rich man tries to buy ancestors. Belus tries to "build himself a name" and, trying to outdo famous estates, becomes bankrupt and loses everything. Pygmalion, seeking fame as the owner of antique statues, dissipates his wealth and sacrifices the welfare of his family to his passion. Most open to satire are the individuals, numerous at court, who try desperately to give the impression that they are having a perfectly wonderful time, how they feel and how they strive "to seem the most transported things alive; . . ." "What bodily fatigue is half so bad?/With anxious care they labor to be glad." Many, to be well known, participate furiously in all fashionable diversions: "The tavern! park! assembly! mask! and play!/Those dear destroyers of the tedious day!" The short exclamatory style suggests in itself the frantic effort to keep in evidence in public association with the great of the court, and it is not a happy life: "None think the great unhappy, but the great."

In contrast with the artificiality and concealed unhappiness of the court, the beauties of the country seem delightful—at first view:

> No splendid poverty, no smiling care,
> No well-bred hate, or servile grandeur, there!
> . . . On every thorn delightful wisdom grows,
> In every rill a sweet instruction flows.

But closer observation discloses much to be satirized: the squire, interested only in hunting, is ill-bred, coarse, ignorant, stupid, and delighted with himself. And at this point, the first satire prepares to end, but not for lack of material. "Ten thousand fools are still in view," as numerous as "lay-atheists made by church debates," or "inconstant ladies," or London citizens who value money above everything, or grave lords subservient to a money lender. The man who is eternally gay, the woman whose tongue "runs for ages without winding up," the writer who has just finished his tenth epic—these might exhaust his theme. But there would always be more: "For who can write so fast as men run mad?"

III   Satire II

Satire II continues with the weaknesses of mankind arising from vanity: "For every soul finds reasons to be proud,/Though hiss'd and hooted by the pointing crowd." With a laugh at those apparently numerous individuals vain of success in the cultivation of unusual flowers—a harmless, and fashionable, folly—Young pictures Florio centering all his joy on his rare tulip:

> From morn to night has Florio gazing stood,
> And wonder'd how the gods could be so good.
> What shape! what hue! was ever nymph so fair?
> He doats! he dies! he too is rooted there.
> O, solid bliss; which nothing can destroy,
> Except a cat, bird, snail, or idle boy.

Though Florio's pride may seem trivial to some, a parallel lack of proportion is seen in excessive value on transitory wealth, fame, or power.

Book-fanciers are satirized. One man feels a passion for "the flower of learning, and the bloom of wit," or at least for the outside of the volumes: "Thy gaudy shelves with crimson bindings glow/And Epictetus is a perfect beau." But this man cares nothing for what is in the books: "Thy books are furniture." Another is eager to possess old, rare books, and goes into debt to buy them—

but he cannot read. Another type of vanity is shown in Hilario,
whose pride is in his wit, and who "spares nor friend nor foe." But,
Young asks, "Who, for the poor renown of being smart/Would
leave a sting within a brother's heart?" He develops this part of his
whole theory of wit, which he is to discuss at greater length in
later writings, and which is in keeping with his announced theory
of satire:

> Then draw your wit as seldom as your sword,
> And never on the weak, or you'll appear,
> As there no hero, no great genius here.
>
> . . . .
> The fame men give is for the joy they find;
> Dull is the jester, when the joke's unkind.

At the other extreme from the wits are those who are "vain of
being dull": "The booby father craves a booby son." Indeed, stu-
pidity is the basis for pride in many affectations and pretensions. A
solemn appearance may merely conceal lack of thought: "Solem-
nity's a cover for a sot."

A man of sense may often "with generous scorn" survey "the
noontide masquerade" of the court and the town where knaves
"hide secure behind a naked face," and where "men talk only to
conceal the mind": "Where generous hearts the greatest hazard
run,/And he who trusts a brother is undone." But extreme concern
for appearance results in absurdities. The satirist has good fun
with the young fop, whose care is all "on outward show," and who
finds happiness and security in fine clothes and rich personal pos-
sessions: "His sumptuous watch-case, though conceal'd it
lies,/Like a good conscience, solid joy supplies." In contrast with
the fop, and yet parallel in his concern for appearance, is he who
might be called the prototype of the modern "beatnik," proud of
looking disreputable: "Their methods various, but alike their aim
—/The sloven and the fopling are the same."

In his concluding lines, satirizing the folly of seeking fame
through poetry, some readers have seen autobiographical expression of personal disappointment:

> Know, fame and fortune both are made of prose,
> Is thy ambition sweating for a rhyme,

> Thou unambitious fool, at this late time?
>
> . . . .
>
> A fool at forty is a fool indeed.

IV Satire III

Satire III turns to a different topic, contemporary learning and literature:

> When wanted Britain bright examples more?
> Her learning and her genius too decays,
> And dark and cold are her declining days.

In lines which echo the feelings Young had earlier expressed and which look forward to his major critical writing, *Conjectures on Original Composition,* he deplores too-great reliance on the past and too-little readiness to welcome originality: "They meanly live on alms of ages past." His satires have both old and new material —the foibles and follies of human beings are not new—but the old has been "New-cast with care, and in no borrow'd mould."

For the regrettable low ebb of literature, the critics are in part to blame; and they invite satire: "For what ambitious fools are more to blame/Than those who thunder in the critic's name?" The first critic to appear in "characteristical" form is Balbutius. In spite of Young's comment that he does not aim at any particular individuals, and though there were many dyed-in-the-wool neo-Classicists, a scholar tends to identify Balbutius with John Dennis:

> Balbutius, muffled in his sable cloak,
> Like an old Druid from his hollow oak,
> As ravens solemn, and as boding, cries,
> "Ten thousand worlds for the three unities."

The greater number of critics, however, lacking basic principles of evaluation, judge from personal reasons: one judges "as the weather dictates; right/The poem is at noon, and wrong at night"; another judges by the author's family connections; "Some judge, their knack of judging wrong to keep;/Some judge, because it is too soon to sleep." But the basic weakness of most critics is that they seek their own fame: "To gain themselves, not give the writer, fame."

Turning to the wider field of miscellaneous seekers for fame, Young mentions the name-droppers, those who want to be thought to know many outstanding persons: "They know a thousand lords behind their back." He suggests that men seek reputation for anything they own—their houses, their paintings, their wives, and even their habits. Vincenna, really proud of himself, affects modesty, "fishing" for compliments, and he haunts "the court without a prospect there." The satirist comments on the fate of such seekers:

> Be wise, Vincenna, and the court forsake;
> Our fortunes there nor thou nor I shall make.
> E'en men of merit, ere their point they gain,
> In hardy service make a long campaign;
> Most manfully besiege their patron's gate,
> And oft repulsed, as oft attack the great,
> With painful art, and application warm,
> And take at last some little place by storm.

A general survey of the country would reveal a picture of a masquerade on a large scale, with artificialities, superficialities, immoralities put before true values. The national enthusiasm for masquerades, a potential evil deplored by others than Young, is a topic for more serious satire and suggests an associated social evil which was fast increasing—gambling. Additional indication of growing corruption is seen in the concern of members of the government, "commons, peers, ministers of state," with the "fate of whores and fiddle-strings" instead of with matters of national import. Here Young defends his tone of Juvenal:

> How terrible it were to common sense,
> To write a satire which gave none offence!
> . . . . The fool and knave, 'tis glorious to offend.

V Satire IV

Satire IV differs from the preceding mainly in presenting several follies in effective, extended character sketches. The first, Chremes, the coffeehouse politician, is reminiscent of the *Specta-*

tor's political upholsterer and is not extinct today. He "drinks his coffee, for the public good," and gives himself to explaining the public situation; he tells what should be done in national and international matters; he foretells what is to happen: "A quid-nunc is an almanack of state." And all this political concern is due to an "incapacity for smaller things." "Poor Cremes can't conduct his own estate,/And thence has undertaken Europe's fate."

His second character, Gehenno, represents another group that Young was much aware of, to which he had referred in *Satire I* as "lay-atheists made by church debates." Gehenno has set himself up in private as an atheist: "Deep in the secret he looks through the whole,/And pities the dull rogue that saves his soul; . . ." But "in public he complies," reserving his "blasphemies" for his friends. While disbelief flourishes among peers in prosperity, "poor rogues run seldom mad." The greatest cure for disbelief is loss of money: "While the sun shines, Blount talks with wondrous force;/But thunder mars small beer and weak discourse."

Another memorable character, one not confined to the eighteenth century, is Narcissus, merely a conforming nonentity. He does everything he thinks he should do: he goes to church regularly; he says nothing in Parliament; he pays his bills! "His character and gloves are ever clean,/. . . A smile eternal on his lips he wears." He attends all social functions:

> Most charitably lends the town his face,
> For ornament, in ev'ry public place;
> . . . And is the furniture of drawing rooms.

Narcissus is indeed "the glory of his race;/For who does nothing with a better grace?" Young has succeeded well in this extended portrait of a colorless individual, always pleasant, and, above all, always present; Narcissus is well designated as one of the "shining expletives of human kind." In striking contrast with such a conformer are those with a passion to be different: "What other men dislike, is sure to please/Of all mankind these dear antipodes." They make a point of defaming celebrated individuals. They take the opposite side in everything, even contradicting elementary facts of nature. These are the single-minded nonconformists.

The collectors form another group inviting to the satirist. They collect all sorts of useless, expensive little objects and "relics":

How his eyes languish! how his thoughts adore
That painted coat which Joseph never wore!
He shows on holidays a sacred pin,
That touch'd the ruff that touch'd Queen Bess's chin.

Lico is a different kind of collector: he collects, or tries to collect, men of title. What, the satirist asks, is the use of such efforts? "Who'd be a crutch to prop a rotten peer?" But he reflects sadly that "the tribe most likely to comply" is none other than "the men of ink":

The writing tribe, who shameless auctions hold,
Of praise, by inch of candle to be sold.
All men they flatter, but themselves the most,
With deathless fame their everlasting boast.

Without inspiration no one should try to write poetry, for no dedication to the great can replace its lack. But, "if talents rare" indicate the ability, then "the crime is to forbear." There are a few "large-minded men" with a genuine interest in poetry who may patronize true worth. This satire ends with a very slightly related tribute to the King for his modesty about his very real military exploits.

VI Satire V

Satires V and VI, each about twice as long as any of the others, turn to that ever favorite subject for satire—women. In both, Young shows a condescension, characteristic of his century, to "the gentler sex." While he does include a few complimentary passages, these usually commend women who are aware of their subordinate intellectual status. *Satire* V is directed largely against silliness, pretenses, and lack of intelligence; and it is presented mainly in brief passages rather than in extended "characters." Ambition in "the fair sex" is mostly expressed in trivia and superficialities, faults which furnish "a fruitful theme," especially as the fair ones are dashing around everywhere with complete lack of discrimination: "As unreserved and beauteous as the sun,/Through every sign of vanity they run." Many of his examples Young gives in sets of contrasts.

Clarinda "burns for fame," seeking it largely through her ability to shift from one emotion to another, "like April suns," all the while looking "delightfully." Zara, on the other hand, never betrays by her cold manner her inward emotions; ostensibly reading the Prayer Book, she is in reality perusing a new play: "Thus gloomy Zara, with a solemn grace,/Deceives mankind, and hides behind her face." Illustrating the idea that women talk too much and should learn to listen, Xantippe, though recommending silence, talks incessantly; true to her name, she readily expresses her ill temper; and, delighting in the sound of her own voice, she must always have the last word in an argument. In contrast, a "gentle nymph," with "peace in her air, persuasion in her eye," is a joy to her husband.

A number of ladies lacking in judgment appear: Sempronia, on the eve of marrying an eminently eligible young man, suddenly marries an old "deform'd, debauch'd, diseased" man who is slightly richer. Lemira, though ill, takes risks by going out to enjoy any diversion, unwilling to miss anything. Lady Cynthia, to be fashionable, stays up all night; and her health suffers. Others, with "curious arts," endeavor to look younger than their years; some secure a variety of effects by change of hair color.

The contrast between nature and art in appearance suggests that between nature in the country and life in town. The beauty of the country, however, has no appeal for Fulvia: she has a passion for the town; fresh air gives her "vapours"; she prefers "smoke and dust and noise and crowds." At this point Young apostrophizes the beauty and quiet of Dodington's Eastbury—where he was writing—and comments that it would never suit the town-lovers.

Phoebe prides herself on her happiness—but always the happiness of yesterday or of tomorrow: "She dares not boast the present hour." Phillis, feeling that present joy should last, demands that her swain's love should be at least eternal: "Eternal love I vow," the swain replies; "But say, my all, my mistress, and my friend!/What day next week th'eternity shall end?"

Seemingly among the ladies most open to satire are those who go in for masculine activities: "They drive, row, run, with love of glory smit,/Leap, swim, shoot flying, and pronounce on wit." Or they aspire to intellectual levels, with an interest in astronomy, theology, or such things outside their proper field. Affectations in manners are distressing: the exaggeration of helplessness at one extreme, and the vigorous coarseness of mannish women at the other. The satire concludes with some good eighteenth-century counsel to the ladies:

> Your sex's glory 'tis to shine unknown;
> Of all applause, be fondest of your own.
> Beware the fever of the mind! that thirst
> With which the age is eminently curst.

VII   Satire VI

Satire VI continues the satire of women's follies with a gradual turning to more serious weaknesses, and it is developed with more extended sketches than appeared in *Satire V*. Lavinia, "polite and not profane," goes to church as regularly as to Drury Lane. "She decently, in form, pays Heaven its due,/And makes a civil visit to her pew." In outward manner she seems very devout, and she reads the words of the Prayer Book with a sweet accent: she is "proud of praying well." With Young's usual fondness for contrasts, he shows us two ladies, different in manner, akin in immorality: Amasia is so free in conduct, so scornful of prudes, so determined not to be thought a saint, so superior to formality that "Some might suspect the nymph not over-good—/Nor would they be mistaken if they should." Abra, all formality, is constantly seen in prayer and engaged in charity: "And this, to do her justice, must be said,/'Who would not think that Abra was a maid?'"

Many examples are given of the fair ladies who delight in making their husbands miserable. They fail to realize that their true beauty and charm rise from "the mind's all-gentle graces" and the light of the soul. Other types are portrayed, such as Aspasia, of high birth and well-bred, who is so very refined that she finds other people awkward and impolite: "She's elegantly pain'd from morn to night." The managing woman, who likes to arrange other people's business and makes involved plans about the simplest matters, is shown in Julia: "For her own breakfast she'll project a scheme,/Nor take her tea without a stratagem." But trifles are after all the province of the fair: ". . . moments make the year/and trifles life." A horrible example of the neglect of personal appearance is given in Alicia, dirty, disheveled, careless:

"Women were made to give our eyes delight;/A female sloven is an odious sight." The picture of the gossip at the ladies' tea table recalls Pope's Belinda and her friends:

> An hecatomb of characters supplies
> The painted altar's daily sacrifice . . .
> Scandal's the sweet'ner of a female feast.

A more serious note now sounds, and Juvenal's satire is more in order to "lash the ranker follies of our age": ladies have taken to drinking; adultery is common; "swarms of amorous grandmothers," "misses, ancient in iniquity," "blasting whispers," "lying, . . . swearing, gaming" characterize the age: " 'Tis not a world, but chaos of mankind." Two only of the long list of evils are exposed at length—irreligion and gambling; and neither is developed in the "characteristical" way used earlier.

On Sundays the lady comes in her finery to church; but she has also an attitude of amused contempt for the doctrine of the Church and prefers the more extreme Deists to St. Paul. She is the "she-atheist," a fashionable development of the day, combining "freedom" in theology with freedom in morals and with a belief that "deity [is] . . . perfectly well-bred" and that evil is the invention of the priests.

Lacking any central foundation for their lives, these ladies need constant diversion; and they find this in the fashionable gaming rooms: "Quadrille has murdered sleep." The tone becomes more serious in this part—incidentally, the longest section dealing with one folly or vice—as the satirist deals with one of the most serious evils of the contemporary fashionable society: "The love of gambling is the worst of ills." He points out some of the resultant evils, and adds anticlimactically, as more telling to the ladies, "And, what is still more dreadful, spoils your face." A somewhat detailed picture of a group of professional gamblers with a lady in their midst, excited by the "game," is followed by a description of the consequent ruin of a family fortune:

> O scene of horror, and of wild despair!
> . . . Why the whole house in sudden ruin laid?
> O nothing, but last night—my lady play'd.

And how, Young asks, is this scene related to the theme of this satire? The ladies who have become victims to the love of gambling began their downward path with "a vain devotion to the mode."

VIII   Satire VII

Satire VII seems in many ways outside the series. It is less "characteristical" than the others and is primarily concerned with satirizing desire of, or celebration of, war, and with the corruption of courtiers. The subjects of the other satires were mainly private follies, often arising indeed from love of wealth and power; but here he is concerned with such passions on a large national and international scale: "The world their field, and human-kind their prey." In the depiction of the madness of war, the first theme, Mars stalks across a world with as much carnage and disaster as ever in the past, "And thrives on mankind's miseries and pains." Young's vivid description of the effect on the beholder of a battlefield just after the battle is effective as part of his anti-war theme and is also interesting as possibly autobiographical. This passage is connected with the theory that Young had visited the Lowlands on business after his father's death and had seen the battlefield immediately after the Battle of Ramillies. If indeed he did, that would account in part for his lifelong anti-war sentiment.

Another passage also possibly has an autobiographical basis. Young points out that evil is done to men not only by those promoting war. Courtiers who "wrap destruction up in gentle words,/And bows and smiles, more fatal than their swords," who deceive basely with false encouragement, who conceal indifference or hostility behind a pretense of friendship, who "coin the face and petrify the heart," and "who give a nod when broken hearts repine" contribute to the unhappiness of many.

Though the catalogue of fools, mentioned in *Satire I*, is now finished, many more remain, says Young, for future satirists: those commentators who interpret only the obvious; critics who show only errors in the Scriptures; misers who ruin young noblemen; lawyers who legally steal; people who laugh at the miseries of others; and other instances of human hardness of heart and dullness of mind. These the satirist leaves to other satirists to whom his effort only "sounds a prelude and points out their prey." But, to complete the design of the whole series, another topic remains: "What is this power whom all mankind obeys?" Love of fame itself seems to be a heaven-sent passion designed to inspire mankind to higher accomplishment: "By large-soul'd men, for thirst of fame renown'd,/Wise laws were framed, and sacred arts were found, . . ." But, when false gods are set up, love of fame becomes no longer a "flaming minister of virtue." Ambition may then be good or bad: in noble minds it is always joined with virtue, but on "meaner minds ambition works alone."

Then, as an example of a man in public life embodying public virtues, Young presents King George II. His praise of the King, Queen Caroline, and Walpole, which forms the concluding lines of this satire, derived in some measure from the situation in which it was written. First published before the death of King George I, it had been dedicated to Walpole, expressing thanks to him for having obtained a pension for him and not asking for anything; and, when, in the 1728 collected edition of the seven satires, he revised it slightly to form the last of the series, he changed the ending, dropping allusion to George I, and bringing it up to date with a reference to George II. There had recently been great national worry about the safety of the King, for, en route to England from Hanover, his ship had been driven into a port in the Lowlands by an unusually terrible storm. In the absence of means of communication it was not known for some time what had become of the royal ship, and in the interval it was believed lost. During that time Queen Caroline as regent and Walpole as leader of the government had carried on for the public welfare. It is to this situation that Young refers in the conclusion of his poem, when he voices the relief of the people and their admiration for those concerned.

Of the dedications to the separate satires, only that to Spencer Compton can properly be called a bid for a patron; and in it Young merely indicates what was indeed true. Compton had held high office and was to hold higher, even though he was not among the ablest men of his time. Young, who overestimated Compton's literary interests, did not make a good choice. Actually, it may have injured him in esteem with the Queen as she supposedly disliked Compton greatly. Young had an unfortunate faculty for getting himself associated with the wrong political figures.

The satires were very successful, not only because of the subject matter but also because of the very effective expression. Heroic couplet, as Dryden had suggested and exemplified in his own writing, is well adapted to satire; and Young's couplets are for the most part concise and pointed, with the rhyme contributing to the witty effect. Many couplets and many single lines are so concise, apt, and witty that they were long quoted and imitated. People enjoy seeing qualities they recognize in others neatly and memorably expressed. Furthermore, Young's indignation at growing corruption in society and his denunciation of war reflected more serious public concerns shared by many. It is interesting to note some variety of contemporary reaction: Swift, more of the school of Juvenal, thought Young's satire not sufficiently biting. A little later an anonymous writer in the *Gentleman's Magazine* thought it had "too many stings." Joseph Warton later wrote of it: "A work that abounds in wit, observation on life, pleasantry, delicacy, urbanity, and the most well-bred raillery, without a single mark of spleen or ill nature. These are the first characteristic satires in our language, and are written in an ease and facility of style. . . ." Dr. Johnson praised it as "a very great performance," in which Young's points have the "sharpness of truth."

The very great success of Young's *Satires* was, however, surpassed by that of Pope's brilliant satires, *Moral Essays, in Four Epistles to Several Persons;* and this fact led to the mistaken conception that Young was an imitator of Pope. Again chronology alone may disprove a misconception: Pope's first "epistle" to be published (now numbered fourth in the completed series) appeared in 1731—six years after the first and three years after the last of Young's. Indeed, in the first satire, Young urged Pope to apply his great abilities to satirizing the abuses of the day: "Why slumbers Pope, who leads the tuneful train./Nor hears that virtue, which he loves, complain?" Apparently with reference to Pope, Young wrote, as he began the second satire, "And, if these strains some nobler muse excite,/I'll glory in the verse I did not write." His later comment that he was leaving a wide field for other satirists may well be considered another invitation to Pope. Pope's satires, though much more biting and personal than Young's, have many verbal echoes from Young,[3] parallels in particular follies and abuses satirized (rather naturally as they were observing the same period), and indeed some resemblance in the basic "key" to men's actions suggested—the "ruling passion" in Pope's and the "love of fame" in Young's satire. Pope would seem to have shown his appreciation of Young's *Satires* by that greatest of compliments —imitation.

The great financial success of the *Satires*—in separate and collected editions—led to a false rumor that long persisted: the story that Young had received a very large sum—or sums—of money from the Duke of Wharton in admiration of the *Satires* is obviously chronologically impossible. Before the first one appeared, Wharton was bankrupt and unable to give anyone gifts of money; and, years before the collected edition, he had left England forever.

Young, like all great satirists with the purpose of leading men to take an objective look at themselves, was concerned not only with the exposure of follies, vices, and evils but also with the potentialities of human nature. He satirized, not love of fame itself, but the means by which men seek it, extremes, affectation, irrationality; and he stressed indeed that ambition, along with other passions, was "heaven-sent" and good or bad as directed. Such a conception of human nature was expressed in many of his later writings; in fact, during the very same years that he was writing some of the *Love of Fame,* he was also busy with his most famous sermon, "A True Estimate," analyzing more deeply the human passions and their propensity to lead to misery through lack of moderation.

CHAPTER 4

The Hedges of Custom: Steps to a New Career, 1722-30

YOUNG'S great problem of the 1720's continued to be the question of his future career. That of a dramatist was at best uncertain; but, though his second play had had less immediate success than his first, he wrote another play, *The Brothers*, which was apparently nearly ready for production in 1724. In a letter of early 1724 to Lady Mary Wortley Montagu,[1] of interest as showing their friendly acquaintance, Young commented on suggestions she had made to improve the play; expressed discouragement in his belief that his play, when acted, "will not more than pay for the paper on which it is written"; and announced his sudden decision to "suppress my play for this season at least," a decision which indicates it was far enough toward completion to have been considered for staging it that year. Two years later Young mentioned in another letter to Lady Mary, written in March, 1726, that Mr. Dodington and the actors approved the play without further change and that he had "more depending on the success of this particular piece than your ladyship imagines." But, while it was in rehearsal, he suddenly withdrew it from production.

For a long time it was believed that his decision had been made because he was considering taking orders in the Church. But letters to Tickell, then in Ireland, written during the 1720's and published in 1931, have thrown further light on the much discussed date of his ordination. Because of a rather long-established custom for the Lord Lieutenant of Ireland to encourage the appointment of clergymen from England to positions in the Church in Ireland, probably for political reasons, it was easier to secure a benefice there than in England. Young, considering the idea of entering the Church and fully aware of how preferments were obtained, had looked into the possibilities in Ireland and had obtained the promise of Lord Carteret, the Lord Lieutenant, that, when three "already on his hands" were taken care of, he would provide for Young. Probably, with a prudent thought that a new play on the stage might be considered inappropriate for a man seeking a church benefice, he had postponed production of *The Brothers* early in 1724. Satisfied from Tickell's letters that the time was ripe, Young proceeded with his plans and presently wrote to his friend that he was then in orders.

On the basis of this letter and its references to events of the time, it has been concluded that Young was ordained on December 22, 1724.[2] He had not taken the step lightly or hurriedly nor, in view of all the facts, was such a step surprising. In the light of his father's brilliant career and his own concern with moral and religious values that is shown so markedly in all his writings, it was only natural that he should become a clergyman. From his years of observation at Oxford and in London, he was familiar with the whole system of church preferment and aware of the vast numbers of ordained men unable to get any benefice. The advisability of making sure of a benefice before ordination was only too apparent. Though it was a most regrettable system, it was beyond his power to change it or to ignore it.

Although Carteret had encouraged Young to hope for rather immediate success, time went by with no such result. In 1726 Carteret renewed his promise, and later in the year he received Young warmly in London. That Young canceled the production of his play, already in rehearsal, at this time, seems to indicate his belief that a benefice was about to be forthcoming. But a few months later Carteret was somewhat vague about the matter, and by the end of 1727 he seemed to disown that he had ever made any promise. This repudiation of promises was by no means unusual; such patrons often found it handy to be lavish with promises for the future and then to deny later that any had been made. But that it was quite usual and that many others were being treated the same way was of little comfort to Young. By 1728 he had given up his empty hopes from Carteret.

During these years of futile expectation of Carteret's favor, Young was busy with a great deal of writing: besides *The Love of Fame,* he did some anonymous writing for periodicals, notably Aaron Hill's new *Plain Dealer;* an important sermon; and a number of poems of an occasional nature. His letters to Tickell show that during the decade he was visiting many old friends: his brother-in-law, John Harris, at Chiddingfold; his Oxford friend Evans at his parsonage in Surrey; and, for long periods, his friend Dodington at Eastbury. And his comments to Tickell on current poetry, that in composition and that newly published, indicate his lively interest in what was going on in literature and in the theater, as well as in the political scene. Concerning the hostility between Walpole and Bolingbroke and "some excellent papers that publicly passed between them," he satirically wrote, "We have had nothing so good on the Stage this season."

I The Instalment

A royal pension of two hundred pounds a year, dated May 3, 1726, but retroactive to the preceding Lady Day, was granted to Young in the name of King George I through Walpole, doubtless influenced by Dodington, at the time devoted to Walpole and very useful to him. Not long afterward Young welcomed an opportunity to express his gratitude to Walpole and to pay tribute to him and to his great achievements as leader of the government—an opportunity afforded by Walpole's being made a Knight of the Order of the Garter, the highest and most coveted honor in the kingdom. Young addressed to him *The Instalment,* a poem which had at least the merit of a timely theme. The occasion of the instalment was a tradition-breaking event: never before had a commoner been admitted to the ancient order, long reserved for warriors and titled aristocrats; moreover, the award for merit as leader of the government was a triumph for the Whigs.

Young's theme of the greatness of Walpole and his own sentiments of gratitude and admiration for Walpole as a great political leader, devoted to peace and preserving it during the difficult international tensions of the 1720's, farsighted in strengthening the navy and the army, and in encouraging commerce and prosperity, were well based—as was his declaration that his "muse" must be devoted to sincerity and sublimity. There need be no quibbling about his sincerity—or enthusiasm; but his efforts for sublimity resulted in highly overstrained expression.

To indicate the suitability of Walpole's admission to the Order, the poem begins with an imaginative picture of all the past knights welcoming the newcomer and adjusting his ceremonial regalia. Mention of the azure ribbon and the star—the emblems of the Order—introduces a series of star symbols to suggest Walpole's greatness: he is the "star" of the government; merging the symbol with that of the North Star, Walpole's skillful steering of "the ship of state" is suggested; next, the association of star and warning comet symbolizes the fear that hostile powers have of the naval might of England; and, finally, in the hint of the possible influence of the stars on the tides, Walpole's part in the granting of the pension is metaphorically presented: "The streams of royal bounty, turn'd by thee,/Refresh the dry domains of poesy." By way of making more "sublime" the designation of Walpole as both an ornament and a profit to the country, he is likened—with ingenuity reminiscent of some of the minor metaphysical poets—to an orange tree: just as it bears flowers and fruit at the same time, so Walpole bears "the fruit of service and the bloom of fame,/matur'd and gilded by the royal beam." In each instance the basic value of the symbol is lost in carrying it too far; "the wind of the poor phrase" is indeed broken "running it thus." The poem ends with reference to the troubled international situation at the moment and to England's power and policy as the main factor in preventing war.

This poem is not one of Young's most effective ones. Indeed, an occasional poem is likely to lose its appeal when the significance of the occasion has no longer any immediacy; but Young himself did not include it in the four-volume collected edition of his works which he "corrected" in his last years. It was added to the fifth volume published in 1773, after the poet's death.

II *"Cynthio"*

A short poem entitled "Cynthio," dated 1727, attributed to Young but not included in his collected works, is also an occasional poem. Addressed to the Duke of Chandos on the death of his son, the young Marquis of Carnarvon,[3] it is written in iambic tetrameter couplets, unlike Young's usual use of heroic couplets. With a good deal of imagery of external nature, it is a rather pleasing poem with suggestions of the imitators of the early Milton—"the vocal grove, the painted mead." Most characteristic of Young are the moral reflection that the chief enemy of virtue is pride and the interest in the new light shed on the nature of the universe by Newton, a subject in which Young showed an ever increasing interest.

The poem begins with eight lines voicing the loss of delight in the beauties and sounds of spring, now that Cynthio is dead; and then, for the next forty-five lines, Young paints scenes of the "wintry waste," the dark night, and "the dark grot" that are more akin to the mood of sadness and melancholy occasioned by the cruelly early death of the young Cynthio. He points out the "prospective joys" which had seemed to lie ahead of the youth; and, in conclusion, indicating hostility to all men of high birth who feel they have special license and to all men of ill nature, he points out the rarity of a man of virtue such as Cynthio.

III *"A True Estimate"*

The sudden death of George I on June 14, 1727, must have been an occasion for some private concern to Young. Would his pension, granted by George I, be continued by George II? Would his position as chaplain to the Princess of Wales merely end now that she was Queen Caroline, or would it lead to something else? The pension was validated for the new reign, but his future as to any church benefice remained in doubt. Late in 1727 he had the opportunity to preach before King George II and Queen Caroline a sermon which he probably hoped might increase his chance of royal preferment. The sermon—expanded into a prose treatise, and printed early in 1728 with the full title of "A Vindication of Providence: or, A True Estimate of Human Life, In which the Passions are considered in a New Light"—is a rather important document in Young's list of writings because it discusses many topics, ideas, and beliefs which find expression not only in his *Satires* but also in his later *Night Thoughts* and in *Centaur Not Fabulous.*

In the treatise, usually referred to as "The True Estimate," dedicated to Queen Caroline doubtless with realization of her interest in theological subjects and of her influence over the King, Young's announced purpose was a justification of Providence, or, in Milton's more famous words, "To justify the ways of God to man." A very carefully organized treatise, the general categories, subcategories, and sub-sub-categories, each numbered, are definitely indicated. His elaborate rhetorical training at Oxford is fully evidenced here. There is especially much use of contrast in illustration, of balanced sentence structure, of parallelism, and of extended metaphor. Although the illustrations are general here and not "characteristical," they frequently recall the characters of the *Satires*.

The Preface comments on the fact that the passions have been a favorite subject of mankind for centuries, as they are basic in human nature; and Young assures the reader of the treatise that he will find "an uncommon variety in it," and that the observations made are "by no means drawn from books but the life," wherein he may find "some traces, some features of his own condition." Unhappily, some of the truths are very "melancholy," but the subject is important to consider, being "that of the nearest, and most general concern to man." His text is: "Set your affections on things above, and not on the earth" (Colloss.iii. 2).

After a consideration of all that is implied in the words of the text, he endeavors "to show the particular method of practising the duty contained in them" by thinking of, judging, and loving "the things above." The complexity of his organization may be indicated by his plan for discussing the difficulty of making choices, of judging: ". . . to avoid confusion in so wide a subject, let us separately consider the different orders, aims, relations, constitutions, tempers, and passions of men; and see this variety in uneasiness and complaint." Each is discussed separately and further divided: "the orders" of men involve consideration of likelihood of happiness or trouble for the peasant, the courtier, the married, the unmarried. He considers, one by one, the "peculiar evils" arising from the respective states of "persons of birth, riches, power, and talents." Next he turns to the "different ages of men," considering the various types of pleasures and satisfactions of young men and of old men, and so on with the other indicated categories. The particular nature of the difficulties of men so categorized is often illustrative of Young's observations of mankind. In considering the various tempers of men, he uses almost proverblike form: "A gloomy temper surveys everything in the worst light, and can discover no blessings." "To the thoughtless and improvident, the surprise of every disappointment doubles the pain." "To the wary and foreboding, the constant expectation of calamity, is a calamity itself."

The discussion of the passions of men forms the main part of the treatise; and, by way of an organizing pattern, he employs a metaphor: the passions "may be considered as so many standard-

bearers, round each of which many mischiefs are ranged in array
against us, and lay waste the tranquility of life." He embarks on a
systematic consideration of the passions as "the pains and promot-
ers of the pains of life": "It is the passions that give the perpetual
motion to human life, that roll us from place to place, from object
to object, nor will the grave itself afford them rest." He considers
each passion with its subsidiary mischiefs, summarizing each discussion with the indicated metaphor: "Love has under its banner,
watching, sickness, abasement, adulation, perjury, jealousy. . . ."
"Fear has under its banner confusion, supplication, servility,
amazement, and self-desertion particularly." "Envy has under its
banner, hatred, calumny, treachery, cabal, with the meagerness of
famine, venom of pestilence, and rage."

Then Young turns to a subject that he believes has not before
been considered: distressing as these passions are in their effect on
mankind, they do not comprise all the dangers to man's happiness; those other passions which are good and pleasurable—com-
passion, indignation, hope, emulation, even joy—are not without
"inconvenience and inquietudes." Even hope sometimes becomes
so impatient that undue delay turns it to despair; joy, if moderate,
is scarcely realized in the "general disquiet of life"; and, if immod-
erate, it is a fever, a tumult, a gay delirium, a transport, "and
becomes a pain." All this, he says, has led some philosophers to see
the main state of happiness in serenity or in indolence, neither of
which is consistent with man's nature and therefore cannot be
happiness. There seems to be no rest for man in this world: "What
therefore, we are to aim at, I shall show in my second discourse."

His next paragraph begins "To conclude on the passions." A
very leisurely conclusion follows, but various loose ends remain.
Topics already discussed prove to have aspects that must be further analyzed—with many interesting comments akin to those in
the *Satires*. He takes "love" as an example and says that it, in
different connections, becomes "voluptuousness, ambition, ava-
rice, or vanity"—four "impulses" which are dominant and "beat
on us, like the four winds of heaven, and keep the restless world in
a perpetual storm." All are "the reverse of that which they pretend
to." Voluptuousness, itself promising pleasure, brings only disappointment; it reduces a man to "the wretched estate of eternally
pursuing and eternally condemning the same things": "The man
of pleasure is the most ridiculous of all beings: he travels with his

ribbon, plume and bells; his dress, and his musick; but through a toilsome and beaten road; and every day nauseously repeats the same track. Throw an eye into the gay world, what shall we see, for the most part, but a set of querulous, emaciated, fluttering, phantastical beings worn out in the keen pursuit of pleasure . . . the thin remains of what is called delight."

Ambition, "like a conflagration, burns on incessant"; constantly eager for more and more, it becomes a form of slavery. An ambitious man never finds happiness; he is "never at home to the present hour, but reaching and grasping at joys to come." The covetous man is never satisfied, and the vain one is "the most distinguished son of folly, and has the most airy happiness of them all. His whole happiness rests with the opinion of others, who scorn and laugh at him."

A backward glance at the discussion so far presents, Young admits, a rather melancholy view of life; and he says that he will close with "a picture of life in miniature" that may be more easily kept in the memory. This miniature picture—somewhat extended —is drawn in elaborate parallel construction. A few examples suffice as illustration: "Where, nothing pleases but in prospect; and to please in prospect only, is not to disappoint alone, but to deride us too. . . . Where, life with most men is to come, till it is past. . . . Where, life is the slave of misery, and yet, most strange and deplorable! the king of terrors is death." He comments truly that almost the whole book of Ecclesiastes may serve as scriptural support of his sermon. He promises that he will at a later date consider in a discourse how some of the miseries which man brings upon himself through his own choices may be "abundantly relieved." Meanwhile the reader is left with but one guiding principle—duty: "I know but one solid pleasure in life, and that is our duty." Although Young never published a second discourse, one might argue that in aspects of his *Night Thoughts* he did provide something of what he had promised.

Young's sermon-treatise has many points of excellence and interest. Unfortunately, for modern taste, it is marred by extreme length; he also expresses some ideas several times; and, though the various expressions are often very skillful, concise, and pointed, the repetition detracts from the cumulative effect. The superior force of the expression of many of the same ideas in the *Satires* may make the reader all the more appreciative of the wit, and gaiety, and pointedness of that poetic work, which is indeed more to the modern taste than any sermon. Yet, read as a formal, serious essay or treatise on ideas of perennial significance, the sermon has much interest. In its own day it was popular: it went through three editions in two years and was included in his collected works. Indeed, Thomas quotes the *Biographia Britannica* as calling it Young's best prose work and as declaring that, if popular support could make one a bishop, Young would have had no difficulty after the publication of "A True Estimate." [4] There is certainly much perennial truth in the "True Estimate" which is perhaps not so much a "melancholy" view of life as a realistic one.

IV   Ocean, An Ode

When in January, 1728, George II in his speech from the throne at the opening of Parliament recommended a series of measures on behalf of the royal navy, Young was prompted to write a poem to the King to celebrate the wisdom of his proposals and the achievements of the navy. The poem, *Ocean, An Ode,* was accompanied by "Discourse on Lyric," a prefatory prose presentation of Young's "idea of perfection in the kind of poem" he was attempting. Though several of his earlier writings indicate his interest in theories of literary criticism, this "Discourse" is his earliest extended discussion and anticipates his much later *Conjectures*. A few passages indicate his central points:

The Ode, as it is the eldest kind of Poetry, so it is more spiritous, and more remote from Prose than any other, in sense, sound, expression, and conduct. Its thoughts should be uncommon, sublime, and moral; its numbers full, easy, and most harmonious; its expression pure, strong, and delicate, yet unaffected; its conduct should be rapturous, somewhat abrupt, and immethodical, to the vulgar eye . . . Fire, elevation, and select thought are indispensable.

And as its subjects are sublime, its writer's genius should be so too; otherwise it becomes the meanest thing in writing, *viz.* an involuntary burlesque.

It is the genuine character and true merit of the Ode, a little to startle some apprehensions.

After naming a number of outstanding ode writers from Pindar to Dryden, with comments on many, he praises Dryden's great *Alexander's Feast,* from which Young had selected a few lines upon which to pattern his own stanza. Then, summing up his ideas of the ode in a passage of sustained contrasts and parallels, he adds: "Above all, in this, as in every work of genius, somewhat of an original spirit should be, at least attempted: . . . Originals only have true life. . . ." As the ancients chose "national and great subjects," so he has chosen one "most proper for an Englishman . . . and (what is strange) hitherto unsung."

The poem itself is of less significance than the "Discourse on Lyric" which preceded it and unfortunately indicated that his theory was better than his practice. In view of the theme, the first eighteen stanzas of dedication to King George were appropriate enough, and the ideas in it and throughout the poem were justified. The qualities praised were to be seen in George; and, too, Young was addressing him not merely as an individual but also as the head of the country—and better George than the Pretender! Furthermore, there was hope in 1728 that the new reign just beginning would be a good one. To be sure, George was not interested in poetry—he declared he did not like "bainting and boetry" —but he did like flattery, and Queen Caroline might read it.

The ode, with its "truly British" theme of the glory of the navy and the commerce of the country, begins with a picture of a peaceful, rural scene beside a calm and "curling" sea, leading to the thought of the sea as the source of wealth and force, commerce and naval strength. The Nereids join in the song of praise. The calm seas tempt all boats to go forth, and terrifying storms toss small boats like so many feathers—but British ships are not dismayed. The beauty of the sea in the light of the stars and the moon, in the glory of the sunset, in the storms or rain or snow, or under the arched rainbow, is suggested in a number of stanzas with rather pleasing imagery. The great wealth from the ocean is like all things transitory, and virtue alone is enduring. "This Britain knows"—and therefore uses the wealth from her ocean trade for public good, for the sort of objectives King George had suggested. The poet foretells increasing naval glory: Britain is a power in the world and that power depends on the ocean.

The timeliness of the theme; the enthusiasm of the poet, which seems to be always aroused by the thought of the sea; the commendable interest in measures proposed for the public good; and many descriptive touches are all very well. Unfortunately, Young, aiming at "sublimity," adopted a metrical and stanzaic pattern which would have defeated any poet: six lines, two of iambic dimeter, a line of iambic tetrameter, then two of dimeter, followed by another of tetrameter, rhyming *aabccb*. The short lines with rhyme close together give a very choppy and monotonous effect, and his overuse of exclamation contributes to make the ode a complete failure. Young's major difficulty seemed to be a lack of any lyric gift. It must be admitted, however, that, though many odes were written at the time, there were very few good ones.

V A Royal Chaplaincy

Whether or not *Ocean, An Ode* had attracted any royal notice, Young's anxiety about his future was doubtless somewhat relieved when on April 30, 1728, he was named as one of the chaplains to King George II. This appointment would necessitate his being on duty at court one month during the year and his preaching the sermon on one of the Sundays. As a general thing, good benefices, prebends, deaneries, and other desirable positions came more readily to royal chaplains than to others. The position also gave an excellent vantage from which to survey the field and know of openings and openings-to-be.

A vivid picture of how the system worked and of the cynical conniving of some royal chaplains for position is revealed in the very interesting—and appalling—correspondence of Dr. Edmund Pyle, whose years as royal chaplain coincide almost exactly with Young's long period in that position. In continued correspondence with a clergyman friend living some distance from London, Dr. Pyle kept him abreast of changing situations, revealed his own schemings and successes in getting better and more positions, and advised his friend on how to do likewise. He had absolutely no illusions about how to get what he wanted. Even when he was not on the immediate lookout for himself, he kept friends in mind, and seemed to watch the whole business as an engrossing national sport.

The terms Pyle used in reference to church appointments indicate his attitude: aware that the Duke of Newcastle not only had control of appointments to bishoprics and the higher positions in the Church, which he managed with political acumen, but also had gained control of lower positions as well, and that he preferred to advance a man whose vacated position could be used for another aspirant to whom he had made promises, Pyle spoke of a transfer to another preferment as a "swop," [5] in the *quid pro quo* system, of "jockeying for preferments" and of "the shuffling of ecclesiastical cards." [6] His advice to his friend is concentrated in one letter: "But if I were in your case . . . I should not sit still . . . ask—say I—with impunity too. If you don't, there are those that will." [7] Of a recommendation for preferment on the basis of eighteen years of service at court, he wrote: "Time will show what this will produce—a man's a fool that is sanguine on such a foundation." Pyle would surely have regarded Young as an idealistic amateur. He was less cynical and calculating than Pyle—and less successful when faced with the same system.

VI Sermon: "Apology for Princes"

Young had an opportunity to attract the attention of some people in power when he was honored by being asked to preach the sermon to the members of the House of Commons on January 30, 1729, the anniversary of the death of Charles I, the Royal Martyr. At such a public commemoration, the official sermon naturally had political significance. Young's sermon, entitled "Apology for Princes, or the Reverence Due to Government," was printed at the request of the House and was then accompanied by a dedication to the Commons urging loyalty and support to the King, the law, and liberty, and stressing the qualities which the members of the Commons ought to have. In the sermon itself Young urged moderation in party controversy and discussed the qualities and duties of the King and those of his subjects: "The life of government is in danger when the majesty, or reverence for it is lost." In his consideration of qualities looked for in the Prince, his suggestion that the good Prince "sends his paternal lustre through the whole royal race" seems to be a tactful reference to the concern over the hostility that was even then seen between George II and Frederick, Prince of Wales. Young spoke against war and pointed out that the glory of past nations had been lost for lack of virtue and religion. In closing, he deplored the current political factions and party strife.

One positive advantage from the opportunity to preach this sermon was that Young, apparently through it, began his lifelong friendship with Arthur Onslow, the Speaker of the House.

VII   Imperium Pelagi

Late in 1729 Young found another opportunity to celebrate the naval power and the commerce of England and to praise the King for diplomatic achievements. In the Continental negotiations to avert war from quarrels over trading rights, George II, well versed in Continental relations, had participated personally, returning home only when success was assured. Young was inspired to write *Imperium Pelagi. A Naval Lyric: Written in Imitation of Pindar's Spirit. Occasioned by his Majesty's Return, Sept. 10, 1729, and the succeeding Peace.* The poem seems to have been published early in 1730.

The Preface, which discusses the Pindaric ode, is of some importance in indicating Young's critical theories which were later to have more elaborate expression:

We have many copies and translations that pass for originals. This Ode I humbly conceive is an original, though it protest imitation. No man can be like Pindar, by imitating any of his particular works. . . . The genius and spirit of great men must be collected from the whole; and, when thus we are possessed of it, we must exert its energy in subjects and designs of our own. . . . Nothing so unlike as a close copy, and a noble original. . . .

The Ode is the most spirited kind of poetry, and the Pindaric is the most spirited kind of Ode. . . .

As he indicated in the Preface, Young divided his poem into five "strains," each preceded by an "argument"—a general indication of the topics to be discussed. Fortunately in the Pindaric ode he chose a more successful stanzaic pattern than in *Ocean,* the slightly longer lines giving a less choppy effect.

An initial picture of a stormy sea, symbolizing apparently the danger and confusion from which the returning King is delivering the country, changes as the topic is opened to a symbolic scene of calm and security. This prelude is developed at length, and with a promise to write without strain or effort:

> I glow! I burn! The numbers pure,
> High-flavour'd, delicate, mature,
> Spontaneous stream from my unlabour'd breast; . . .

Then in the various "strains" he rejoices in the possibilities of greater commerce because hampering international difficulties have been removed; introduces as a Pindaric digression a picture of the fall of Tyre to warn against corruption; discusses Britain's strength and spirit of liberty, her far-flung commerce, the significance of trade in opening up relations with far distant lands, and the need for concern for human welfare. In the "Close," he points out the novelty of treating his theme in poetry instead of prose and its suitability for the Pindaric ode.

The poem is overlong and overstrained in reaching for sublimity, and, though Young's enthusiasm for his subject is sincere, his success in lyric is not much greater than that in *Ocean*.

VIII   *In Search of a Benefice*

As the months went by, Young's hopes that the royal chaplaincy would lead to a benefice were not realized. Following the example of scores of others seeking some kind preferment, he wrote a letter to Mrs. Howard, asking her to use her influence on his behalf with the King. Because this letter, not in itself important, in later years caused such a to-do among his nineteenth-century detractors, it is well to consider it briefly.

Mrs. Howard, later Countess of Suffolk, as one of the Women of the Bedchamber to Caroline, Princess of Wales, had attended her in their later court after the Prince's quarrel with the King. Mrs. Howard was very popular with the pleasure-loving people who flocked to the Prince's estate at Richmond. She too had property there which she landscaped with the advice of Pope, who, along with many of his friends, admired her greatly. When the new reign began, she remained as one of Queen Caroline's ladies; as mistress of the King, she was believed to have influence over him politically, and her apartments at St. James were thronged with applicants for help in securing positions, pensions, and other marks of royal favor. Jonathan Swift too sought preferment through her, and blamed her for not securing it. As a matter of fact, she had no political influence at all with George II.[8]

At the end of 1729, or early in 1730, when Young wrote to her, he set forth his qualifications as to abilities, manners, service, want, age, suffering, and zeal for His Majesty. His petition was as fruitless as similar petitions made to her by Swift, Gay, and a vast number of others. That Young should appeal to the King's mistress was very disturbing to the moral sensibilities of some people in the nineteenth century who knew nothing of her social prestige and of the friendship and admiration she had from many eminent men of her time. Actually Young's mistake—and that of others—was in overestimating her influence.

It should be kept in mind that Young, in seeking a benefice, was trying to get a position where he could function as a clergyman with his own church, where he could establish a home and marry. Such effort is no more appropriately branded as "place seeking," with sneering overtones, than it is today for a man, having finished preparations for college teaching and secured the doctoral degree, to look for a position in a college or university. Nor today does one consider this man reprehensible if, having become an instructor, he looks for advancement and a better position elsewhere. Furthermore, a man must bear in mind the "hedges of custom" of his own time and place.

IX *Two* Epistles to Pope

Young's continued disappointment in his hopes for a benefice did not, however, lead either to gloomy self-pity or to withdrawal from other interests. Some of his time went to the writing of two poems more in the spirit of his great *Satires* than his more recent odes on public matters. In a letter to Tickell in February, 1728, he had commented on the progress of Pope's "Burlesque Heroick on Writers"—" 'tis near done and what is done is very correct." When the *Dunciad* appeared late in the year, it met with great admiration but a storm of fury from many, chiefly those who felt themselves victimized by Pope. Young was one of the admirers, and his *Epistles to Pope* appeared early in 1730.

Epistle I, agreeing that the people satirized deserved Pope's treatment, is largely in the vein of Young's own satires. It begins with a picture of Pope peacefully occupied at Twickenham, planning additions to his celebrated garden or reading "the volumes of the wise and good," while in London a journalistic storm rages, and "at parties, parties brawl": "Letters, essays, sock, buskin, song,/And all the garrets thunder on the throng!" Young feels that he must write against all the horde of Grub Street writers who denounce Pope. Then, in the manner of his *Satires,* he indicates a vast throng of types of individuals inviting satire:

> The college sloven, or embroider'd spark;
> The purple prelate, or the parish-clerk;
> The quiet *quidnunc,* or demanding prig.

England is indeed a land of liberty—for all to write who feel the urge. Some write from boredom or frustration; some, from dissatisfaction with the weather or the public situation. With his "characteristical" method, Young shows Lico—without learning, humor, or ability—starting to write—nonsense:

> In immortality he dips his quill;
> And since blank paper is denied the press,
> He mingles the whole alphabet by guess, . . .

He satirizes mercenary writers who are used by politicians and then discarded; hirelings who write poisonous falsities at the dictation of their employers; writers who corrupt by undermining religion. The country, he says, is full of "the poor and the profligate" who have rallied to attack the *Dunciad.* This satiric letter, in which he so enthusiastically seconds Pope's attack on dullness, recaptures the manner and verve of his own *Love of Fame,* and a number of his lines were to be echoed by Pope in his *Epistle to Dr. Arbuthnot.*

Epistle II, written from Oxford, "where the cause of poetry should be most supported," focuses attention on writers and good writing: "Serious should be an author's final views;/Who write for pure amusement, ne'er amuse." Bidding the would-be writer to consult the great authors of the past for advice, he points out that the poet, no less than the priest, should be a man of virtue; that wit is not necessary but "plain sound sense" is. Agreeing with Horace, he urges the writer to "excuse no fault":

> Write and rewrite, blot out and write again,
> And for its swiftness ne'er applaud your pen.
>   .   .   .   .

> Do boldly what you do, and let your page
> Smile, if it smile, and if it rages, rage.

But the poet should not be too devoted to satire. He should be the friend of his king, his country, truth, religion. Should he write satire, he should avoid personal attacks:

> 'Tis dull to be as witty as you can.
> . . . As the soft plume gives swiftness to the dart,
> Good-breeding sends the satire to the heart.

Unless the poet has something new to say, he should not write: "If naught peculiar through your labours run,/They're duplicates, and twenty are but one." Young sums up his advice to writers:

> Weighty the subject, cogent the discourse,
> Clear be the style, the very sound of force;
> Easy the conduct, simple the design,
> Striking the moral, and the soul divine:
> Let nature art, and judgment wit, exceed!
> O'er learning reason reign; o'er that, your creed!
> Thus virtue's seeds at once and laurels grow; . . .

The lasting quality of a piece of writing can be proved only by time, but there will be "snarlers" who seek to "wound immortals, or to slay the slain."

X *End of a Period*

During the decade of the 1720's Young had been away from Oxford on leave of absence often and for long periods, but he retained his close ties with his college and his many friends there. His fellow's rooms at All Souls had remained his home for twenty years, and there he had done much of his writing. Late in the fall of 1729 he returned there after an extended absence and remained till midsummer. Then, at long last, after many disappointments since his ordination in 1724, he was granted a benefice, not through political channels, but "in the gift of the Warden and Fellows of All Souls," as rector of Welwyn, Hertfordshire, on July 30, 1730; and he was officially installed on November 3. This event marks the beginning of a new period in Young's life.

CHAPTER 5

Life's Vicissitudes: Welwyn, 1730-50

IT must have been a tremendous satisfaction to Young to have at last a church of his own and an opportunity to make a home. The beginning of the decade of the 1730's seemed to promise a new period of happiness. Welwyn itself had many advantages: a pleasant parish of about twelve hundred people, twenty-two miles from London on the great North Road to York, it offered opportunity for quiet meditation, enjoyment of outdoors, and cultivation of a garden; and, at the same time, it was not an isolated spot and was easily accessible to London. The benefice was considered a good one, with an annual stipend of three hundred pounds and a rectory. This income, with his pension, royal chaplaincy, and monies from his writing, offered sufficient financial security for him to marry; and there was also a possibility that his claims on the Wharton estate, which he had presented early in 1730 at a hearing before the Master of the Rolls, might someday be paid.

In a letter to Thomas Tickell in 1726, congratulating him on his marriage, Young had expressed a wish that he could afford to marry. In his "True Estimate" he had weighed the advantages and disadvantages of marriage in relation to human happiness: "The married state only may be the most happy, but it is the most dangerous. . . . The state of celibacy, unless it can work out as artificial happiness from the absence of evils . . . is a desert, melancholy, and disconsolate state."

On May 27, 1731, he was married to Lady Elizabeth Lee. The marriage proved successful and gave promise of a whole new life of rich companionship and happiness. Socially, it was a very good one; for Lady Elizabeth was a member of a family with many prominent connections, friends, and contacts at court. The widow of her cousin, Colonel Francis Lee, who had died in March, 1730, she was herself the younger daughter of Edward Henry Lee, the

first Earl of Lichfield, and his wife Lady Charlotte Fitzroy, a natural daughter of Charles II and the Duchess of Cleveland. Young
had perhaps met Lady Elizabeth when at court as royal chaplain.
In marrying Dr. Young, she married a gentleman bearing a family
coat of arms, a poet with a considerable reputation, a royal chaplain who might well expect high preferment, and a clergyman
with a rather good benefice, comfortably accessible to London
and to Ditchley, the family home of her brother, the second Earl
of Lichfield. That she was not personally wealthy is indicated in a
letter of Mrs. Delany commenting on her widowhood: "Poor
Lady Betty is very much to be pitied, for she is left with three
children to maintain, and not a farthing to support her." [1] Later in
1730, however, her position had been somewhat relieved by a
royal grant of a hundred pounds per year in recognition of the
services of her late husband.

The exact age of the three Lee children at the time of her marriage to Young is not known. Elizabeth was probably around
twelve at least, as she was to marry in four years; Charles Henry
was under eleven;[2] and Caroline, goddaughter and namesake of
the Queen, was the youngest. Young was very fond of his stepchildren, and the relations between them were close. Cordial relations with Lady Betty's brother and later with her nephew, the
third Earl, are evidenced by letters throughout the years. The
young Charles Henry Lee was well looked out for by his various
uncles at court; and, even as a young child, he immediately succeeded to his father's title of Master of the Revels; and, in subsequent years, he held various positions at court. To the end of his
life he remained devoted to Young.

As the rectory proved too small for his new family, Young
bought a house near by, known as "Guessens," a house which was
to be his home the rest of his life and a center of hospitality to
many friends. Many improvements to the grounds and the garden
were made gradually over the years. Getting established in his
new home and work must at first have taken much of his time, for
he was evidently a conscientious clergyman.

In June, 1732, his only child was born in Somerset House, London; and at his baptism Frederick, Prince of Wales, was his godfather, and the Prince's name was given him. Whether this honor
was due to Dodington's influence, as he was a close associate of
the Prince, or to the influence of Lady Betty's family is not cer-

tain. This occasion occurred a few years before the sensational quarrel between the Prince and his father, George II; and no one could have foreseen then that connection with Frederick would become detrimental to favor at the royal court. But the honor done Young by Frederick doubtless contributed to the obstacles to Young's preferment in later years.

I *Two Odes of the 1730's*

The 1730's were years of international tension. Early in the decade the shifting European alliances to which Hanover was especially sensitive and the possibilities of danger to British trade and British control of Gibraltar seemed to threaten the peace of the country. Walpole's anti-war policy became increasingly unpopular. Young, a supporter of Walpole and an enthusiastic admirer of the naval power of Britain, was moved to write a poem, *A Sea Piece. In Two Odes*, 1733, reminiscent in many respects of his *Ocean, An Ode* of 1728, and *Imperium Pelagi* of 1730. In the dedication to Voltaire he contrasts Voltaire's use of heroic deeds of the past for epic themes with his own present theme of contemporary British naval might, and recalls their acquaintance in bygone years at Eastbury.

The first ode, "The British Sailor's Exultation," questions the reasons for the rumors of war and cites the power of the navy as a strong deterrent. With enthusiasm, the poet describes the building of the great wooden warships and the production of vast armaments; and he warns other nations against provoking war. In detail he pictures the fury of modern naval battle. The second ode, "In Which is the Sailor's Prayer before Engagement," gives a hypothetical sailor's prayer as a means of expressing the aims of Britain should war come. In both odes, Young shows his fondness for imagery of the sea and for Classical mythology, his awareness of the national situation, and his support of the anti-war policy. They are both written in the stanzaic pattern of *Imperium Pelagi* and show again, unfortunately, his ineptitude in the lyric form.

The next year, 1734, he wrote a continuation or second form of the *Sea Piece*, under the title *The Foreign Address*, with a descriptive subtitle: "Occasioned by the British Fleet, and the Posture of Affairs when Parliament Met." This work is a very curious kind of ode in that much of the 1733 ode is incorporated in it practically unchanged. The argument is developed at much greater length, in the same metrical pattern, with much of the same imagery—and with no greater success. Whether or not the closing lines, "Adieu, pacific lyre . . . ," indicate a conscious taking leave of the ode form, this was his last ode. Indeed, except for an epitaph, this was his last poem before, some eight years later, Young began to publish his greatest work, the *Night Thoughts*.

II *Vicissitudes*

The year 1735 saw the beginning of a change in the pleasant home in Welwyn. The young Elizabeth Lee was married to Henry Temple, eldest son and heir to Viscount Palmerston; but the promising happiness of the marriage was not to last long. Within a year the young wife, always delicate, had developed tuberculosis; and, in an effort to save her life, Young, Lady Betty, and Henry Temple set off with her for Nice. On the way she became worse and died at Lyons on October 8. As the Roman Catholic Church forbade burial of a Protestant in the cemetery, other arrangements had to be made; and she was buried in the "old burial-ground of the Hôtel-Dieu at Lyons," known as the cemetery of the Swiss colony. As was customary, the funeral was at eleven o'clock at night. It must have been an unusually distressing situation, with the death of the young wife and daughter so far from home, under trying circumstances of travel, and with the difficulties in arranging for the funeral.

Young and Lady Betty proceeded to Nice for much of the winter because of her frail health. The two Lee children, Charles Henry and Caroline, and little Frederick Young were doubtless with some of their mother's family, very likely at Ditchley, where they seem to have visited from time to time. On the way home later on, Young was himself taken ill; and at the end of 1737 he made his first visit to Bath for his health. References to sickness are frequent in his letters of subsequent years.

Two letters of 1739 [3] give a glimpse of his stay at Nice, where on fine days he had walked much by the sea and had also enjoyed meditation in quiet shade: "When I was there, I contracted a great intimacy with the Mediterranean. Every day I made him a solemn visit. . . . If you visit my quondam habitation, you will pass a solemn assembly of cypresses; I have a great regard for their memory and welfare." His correspondent, John Williams, a rather freethinking acquaintance of former years, was not the

kind with whom Young would have shared private memories; but
certainly one may read between the lines and feel that on these
walks he thought much about the death of his stepdaughter and
the delicacy of his wife.

Williams had evidently included in his letter a hope that by this
time Young had become a dean or a bishop, deeming it natural
that he would have received such preferment. Turning from some
serious good advice, Young replied in a rather jesting tone: "But
why this sermon? to show myself qualified for the deanery or
mitre you so kindly wish me. But these things are long in coming.
If in your travels you should pick me up a little vacant principal-
ity, it would do as well; I am as well qualified for it, and as likely
to succeed in it. Monaco would be a pretty sinecure. . . ." His
jesting comments do not seem to indicate a burning desire for
preferment.

An indication of the interest in Young's poetry in the same year
is cited by Shelley (pp. 113–14). Edmund Curll, a publisher with
a somewhat notorious reputation in the book world, who occasionally sought to improve his standing by printing reputable
books, wrote to Young proposing a collected edition of his writings and asking for Young's co-operation for advertising purposes.
Though unwilling to be associated with Curll, Young could not
forbid the publication as there was no legal protection against
piracy of such writing. In his three letters in reply to Curll's com-
munications, he merely suggested that he felt it a mistake to omit
the paraphrase of Job, that he was not "at leisure to review what I
formerly writ," and that the *Epistle to Lansdowne* (of which he
said he had no copy) and the *Oration on Colonel Codrington*
could well be omitted: "I think your collection will sell better
without them." Curll published the collected edition in 1741, with
the title, *Dr. Young's Pieces;* and, with his customary disregard for
truth, he advertised it as "made by his approbation and under his
own direction."

The lack of leisure Young had mentioned in December was
doubtless connected with Lady Betty's long illness. On January 29,
1740, she died. Her death was perhaps the greatest blow of his life,
and letters over many years give evidence of his deep and lasting
grief. On returning to Welwyn after an absence, he wrote to the
Duchess of Portland late in 1740: "I have been above ten days at
this place, where my memory is very troublesome to me, and my

understanding is hard put to it to get the better of its severe imper
tinence" (*Bath MSS*, p. 256). In the following July, in a letter to
her on the death of her father, he wrote: "I too well know that the
first agonies of real sorrow have no ears, and that a man might as
wisely talk with his friend in a fever, and desire his pulse to be
still as to philosophize with a wounded heart" (*Bath MSS*, p. 262).
His letter of January 12, 1742, seems to have bearing on his own
bereavement: "There is but one objection against marriage, and
that is one which the wise world amongst its ten thousand objec-
tions never makes; I mean that the husband and wife seldom die
in one day, and then the survivor must be necessarily miserable"
(*Bath MSS*, p. 262).

The opening lines of the sixth poem in the series of *Night
Thoughts* were evidently written with the long illness of Lady
Betty in mind, a long descriptive passage epitomized in two lines:
"The longer known, the closer still she grew;/And gradual parting
is a gradual death." Many years later, on February 7, 1759, in a
letter to the German poet Klopstock about the death of his wife,
Young indicated how lasting was his own grief at losing Lady
Betty: "I can not lay my pen aside, without my heart condoling
your very, very great loss. I am too well qualified so to do, having
not long ago, undergone the same Calamity.—I say, not long ago;
for tho' it is many years since, yet the wound was so deep, that it
seems even now recent, and often bleeds, as if it had been received but yesterday." [4]

The year 1740 marked, indeed, the end of one period with the
death of his wife in January and with the news in April of the
death of his close friend of over thirty years, Thomas Tickell. It
also marked the beginning of a decade filled with problems and
changes in his Welwyn home; old and new legal matters; the addition of many new friends, hopes and disappointments; and,
most of all, it was the period of his greatest achievement in poetry.

III   *Family Changes*

The death of Lady Betty, only four years after that of Elizabeth
Lee, made Welwyn a place of poignant memories, and it is little
wonder that the year 1740 saw Young making many brief trips
away. In March, when the financial claims on the Wharton estate
were being considered in the Court of Chancery, he was called to

London to answer questions concerning the claims which he had submitted in 1730; and, as the matter dragged on, he was obliged to make several other visits to London. The question of the administration of Lady Betty's property was held up in the court for a year; but it was not until the end of October, 1743, that a decision in the Wharton case disallowed Young his original annuity, but allowed a second annuity which had been granted to replace the first unpaid one and dismissed the bond for expenses and losses connected with the election in which Wharton had involved him. Whether or not the arrears in the long unpaid annuity were paid remains uncertain.

Personal loneliness at Welwyn, the problem of a young child not yet eight years old at the time of his mother's death, and the need for someone to take charge of the household presented many difficulties. It may have been during his March visit to London that he met Mrs. Judith Reynolds, the sister of Sir James Reynolds, and began soon after to consider the possibility of providing a mistress for his household by a second marriage. The letters written to her[5] over a period from May 21, 1740, to February 27, 1741, show a rather coldly respectful attitude and a businesslike intention of making everything clear beforehand as to the responsibilities that would be hers, as well as a discreet desire to keep the matter entirely private until the final settlement. The variety of places from which the letters were written affords evidence of his whereabouts during these months. It is of interest that he went to Ditchley to consult his brother-in-law, the Earl of Litchfield, about the idea and that he then went to East Sheen to discuss it with Henry Temple, to whom he was devoted and whom he regarded as his son-in-law as affectionately as before Elizabeth's death and Henry's remarriage. It is in a letter to Mrs. Reynolds that we have his expression of great grief at the untimely death of Henry Temple in August, 1740. As Sir James Reynolds was not in favor of the marriage, the matter was dropped with polite thanks and best wishes. There was certainly nothing unusual about considering a second marriage. Lady Betty had married a second time, as had Henry Temple.

The solving of the problem of the little boy brought another significant change. After necessarily fairly long preliminaries, Frederick at the unusually early age of ten entered Winchester College in November, 1742, as a scholar, just as his father and grandfather had done many years before. Sending the child away to school indicates no lack of feeling on Young's part. The only educational alternative would have been instruction by a tutor at home, and he believed that any advantages of such private education were outweighed by those afforded by the great public schools. His fondness for children is shown by his love for his stepchildren and their devotion to him; his many loving inquiries about the children of the Duchess of Portland, his affection for the young daughters of Samuel Richardson and the pleasure they found in visiting "the good Dr. Young" at Welwyn all indicate that he liked and was liked by children and young people. His tenderness for his own little son must have been equally great.

During the next nine years, until entering Oxford, Frederick was to be under the firm discipline of Winchester College, spending at most the twice-a-year vacations at home, or with his mother's family at Ditchley or his father's relatives at Chiddingfold, quite near Winchester. In all probability his father visited Winchester, where he had strong ties, occasionally during those years too. The absence of extant letters or records concerning Frederick until 1750, though much to be regretted, in no way can be taken to indicate any lack of family devotion. Young was doing his best for his son, and Frederick was leading the normal life of a boy of his social level.

While Young visited many different places in 1740, it is not necessary to conclude that he was away from home continuously during the year. He could go from Welwyn to East Sheen, Ditchley, Bulstrode, London, or Tunbridge Wells in a relatively short time on horseback or by coach. As yet he had no curate, though he might on occasion arrange for a substitute clergyman for his church. June was his regular month of duty as royal chaplain, and later in the summer he was in such poor health that he went to Tunbridge Wells "to drink the waters"; and he then began the practice of an almost annual "cure" there.

IV   *Letters to the Duchess*

Of all the changes in Young's life in 1740 perhaps the most rewarding to him was the addition of many new friends, especially the Duchess of Portland and several of her friends. It was at Tunbridge Wells that his earliest extant letter to her was written on August 25. The correspondence had begun before this date, for in his letter he mentions a previous one written when he was "extremely ill"; and he accepts with great pleasure her invitation to visit her at Bulstrode. Just how he became acquainted with her is not known; but, considering her rank, the initiative must certainly have come from her. A warm and lasting friendship began between the Duchess, then twenty-five, and the poet, fifty-seven.

His letters to her from 1740 until a few weeks before his death have become one of the most valuable sources of information about him. Fortunately she treasured them. Years later, on December 2, 1753, Mrs. Delany wrote: "I have had great entertainment too from Dr. Young's letters to the Duchess, which she has been settling, and read me above three score. They are I think the best collection of men's letters I ever read: strong sense, fine sentiments, exalted piety, they are written with as much ease and freedom as politeness can admit of to a great lady, and the compliments are delicate, without the least flattery . . . and for wit, and lively and uncommon imagination he is most excellent." [6]

The Duchess of Portland, as the daughter of the second Earl of Oxford and Lady Cavendish Holles, the first cousin of the powerful Duke of Newcastle, was connected with many outstanding, influential families. As a child, Margaret Cavendish Harley had been admired by the many poets and men of letters who were her father's friends; and, at five, she was Prior's "noble, lovely little Peggy." In 1734 she had married William Bentinck, the second Duke of Portland, also of an influential Whig family. At their great country estate, Bulstrode, famous for its magnificence and beautiful gardens, she entertained on a large scale. The Duchess, intelligent, accomplished, and of a warm, outgoing nature, enjoyed trying to improve the situation of her friends through the great influence of her family connections; and, at the time of Young's first visit, she had been endeavoring to advance Mrs. Pendarves at court through Lord Baltimore's influence on Lord Lansdowne.

Mrs. Pendarves, formerly Mary Granville and later Mrs. Delany, was the niece of Lord Lansdowne, who had arranged her first unhappy marriage. She had known Lady Betty Lee at court some years before her marriage to Young; and Lady Betty's nephew, the young Lord Baltimore, had been at the time much enamored of her. She may well have met Young too before 1740. Their friendship was to last until the end of his life; and, after her

marriage to Mr. Delany about 1744, he also became Young's devoted friend. Her autobiography and letters, which afford valuable, fascinating accounts of eighteenth-century life at many
levels, make many references to Young and his poetry. She herself
was a charming and talented lady, with a wide range of interests.
For a time at the end of 1740 the Duchess seems to have had some
hopes of effecting a marriage between the widowed Mrs. Pendarves and Young.

The much anticipated first visit to Bulstrode was evidently most
enjoyable for him. There he also met the twenty-year-old Elizabeth Robinson, whom he remembered seeing at Bath on his visit
there a few years before. She later became Mrs. Montagu and
remained a lifelong friend of Young's; and, thanks to her letter-
writing abilities, one has many glimpses of him over the years.
Before he arrived at Bulstrode, she wrote to her sister of her
eagerness to see him: "We wish for his coming, for I hear he is
agreeable, and, indeed, his private character is excellent." That
she was not disappointed in her expectations appears in her next
letter: "I am much entertained with him, he is a very sensible
man, has a lively imagination, and strikes out very pretty things in
his conversation." And to her mother she wrote that, ". . . as for
Dr. Young, he is a very sensible man, and an entertaining companion, and starts new subjects of conversation, and there is nothing so much wanted in the country as the art of making the same
people chase new topics without change of persons." [7]

Elizabeth's friend, Mrs. Donellan, who met Young later at Tunbridge Wells, voiced the same admiration of his conversational
abilities: "I conversed much with Doctor Young, but I had not
enough to satisfy me. We ran through many subjects, and I think
his conversation much to my taste. He enters into human nature,
and both his thoughts and expressions are new." [8] In replying to
her friend, Elizabeth wrote: ". . . there is nothing of speculation,
either in the Terra Firma of Reason, or the Visionary province of
Fancy, into which he does not lead the imagination. In his conversation he examines everything, determines hardly anything, but
leaves one's judgment at liberty." [9]

Something of the variety of Young's letters,[10] as indicated in
Mrs. Delany's praise in later years, may be illustrated by a few
examples from the letters of 1741. In a letter in February he proposed a way to make the company of dull or disagreeable persons

enjoyable: "If then, Madam, Dr. ——— and Mrs. ——— should visit us, let us suppose ourselves in the theatre, and that the parts of an oaf and a vixen were represented before us, how then should we admire the wonderful talents of the performers, and swear every word, air, and action, was acted to the life, and thus steal from a visit the best dramatic entertainment we ever saw, without the expense of a crown" (*Bath MSS*, p. 261).

In an entirely different vein he wrote a long letter to her some little time after her father's death: "Heaven suffers nothing to happen to man but what is for his temporal or eternal welfare, and our fears have as much reason to praise God as our triumphs. . . . . Heaven is as solicitous for our happiness here, as is consistent with its far kinder concern for our happiness hereafter, and our afflictions . . . plainly tell us we are immortal; were we not, we should be as destitute of hopes too, as the beasts that perish" (*Bath MSS*, p. 262).

Another letter written in a less serious mood shows his satiric pleasure in observing the follies of mankind at Tunbridge Wells: "There is a great fortune, which is followed by a pack of noble beagles, but which shall be the happy dog no one can tell." And in a mock serious tone he replied to an invitation to pay a second visit to Bulstrode: "To be courted by a Duchess in my old age is a very extraordinary fate. Should I tell it to my parishioners, they would never believe one word I spoke to them in the pulpit afterwards: I lie therefore under a terrible dilemma; I must either burst by stifling this secret, or make atheists of my whole neighborhood." (*Bath MSS*, p. 263).

Many of his letters contain little more than comment on people in general and on situations of interest to the Duchess or serious reflection on some thoughts of his. At one time she had said that she did not like personal chitchat in letters, but one regrets that he did not write more about himself and his family. Though he evidently discussed poetry in conversation with her, he did not do so in his letters. Nor apparently either in letters or conversation did he mention any writing in progress.

During the decade of the 1740's one of the most important friendships of his life began to flourish. Just where and when he first met Samuel Richardson is not certain, but it may well have been many years before, when Richardson was printing the periodical which the Duke of Wharton had started, or it may have been through their mutual friend, Arthur Onslow, the Speaker of the House of Commons. Young admired Richardson's *Pamela* and followed the development of *Clarissa* with interest. Just as, in bygone years at Oxford, Young and Tickell had discussed their poetry together, so now Young and Richardson shared many intellectual interests and freely expressed their opinions about each other's writings. Their extant correspondence extends from 1744 to Richardson's death in 1761, and they also saw each other often during the years.

A few references to his stepchildren, which occur in Young's letters of the 1740's, afford glimpses of his devotion to them. Mention of Caroline's visits to London, of Young's pride in the Duchess's complimentary comments on her, of his dependence on her as director of his household in his saying he could not leave Welwyn at one time until she returned from a visit, and of messages of thanks from Caroline for kindnesses to her indicate what a place she filled in his daily life. A letter of late September, 1743, written in a rather gay tone, announced that he was about to officiate at the wedding of a fine young man whom he said she might know—Charles Henry Lee. About four months later, January 24, the young man died. Young wrote to the Duchess of the blow to Caroline: "Next to his poor wife, she is the greatest sufferer, an only sister, and most beloved."

Letters during the next few years also show his devotion to Caroline: he mentioned visits they had made together to Richardson's home; he worried over danger to her from smallpox in the neighborhood; he was concerned over her engagement to an army officer, and had her consult the head of the Lee family, her cousin, the third Earl of Lichfield, and her uncle, Admiral Fitzroy Lee; he worried about her worry during the Jacobite rising of 1745 when her fiancé, Major Haviland, was stationed at Stirling Castle right in the path of the invading Highlanders. After her marriage early in June, 1748, the couple stayed at Welwyn with him for several months, delayed by army orders and by a lawsuit over her brother's estate. When they left for Ireland, Young, anxious lest army life prove too much for her somewhat delicate health, wrote to friends there on her behalf. Late in 1749 Caroline, still in her twenties, died in Ireland; but no letter of Young's is extant telling of his last blow.

Throughout this busy decade Young's letters to the Duchess afford many glimpses of the hospitality at Welwyn: at one time he had "a houseful of guests"; at another he spoke of a cozy group enjoying conversation around an open fire while the wintry winds blew outside; again someone was coming to spend the summer; and very often individual friends dropped in for briefer visits. His identification with the interests of Welwyn was shown by improvements he had made—the establishment of "assemblies" and a bowling green for the social enjoyment of his parishioners; the redevelopment of the Welwyn Waters, which he described as similar to those of Tunbridge Wells; and the building of a new steeple on his church. His participation in local affairs as a member of the assizes to prevent the spread of "the murrain" among the cattle prevented him from accepting invitations to Bulstrode. His benevolence and sympathy for people in difficulties and his efforts to do something for them were frequently reflected.

Mrs. Montagu's letters provide several glimpses of him, especially at Tunbridge Wells during his annual "cures." On one occasion she was astonished, and seemingly somewhat shocked, to find him enjoying conversation with Colley Cibber, whom Young had known from many years before and whose reminiscences of his colorful past life in the theater must have proved most interesting. When Young learned from the Duchess that Mrs. Montagu had written to her about her surprise, he replied with some amusement that, while Colley showed many follies, "his morals shall not hurt me"; and he suggested that Mrs. Montagu had shown some prudery in her attitude. Mrs. Montagu and Young seemed always to find pleasure in each other's company in spite of their great difference in age. On one occasion she, another friend, and Young had ridden some five miles from Tunbridge Wells to see some ruins. She described the whole expedition with a good deal of witty and entertaining exaggeration, especially their conversation with a humble parson at a church near the much admired ruins. The contrast between the comical terms in which she pictured the poor man and her condescending attitude to him and the consideration and courtesy shown by Young are evident in her account. In the serious latter part of her letter she described their return to Tunbridge Wells by moonlight, and wrote that Young, the only one who spoke, from time to time "uttered things fit to be spoken in a Season when all Nature seems to be hushed and hearkening." [11] Doubtless some of the thoughts of his recently completed *Night IX* contributed to his conversation.

V *Efforts for Preferment*

A new and important topic, which was to concern them both for many years, appears in Young's letter written to the Duchess on August 1, 1742, in reply to her letter telling him that she and the Duke of Portland had started steps to secure church preferment for him and had approached the two most important persons concerned with such matters, the Duke of Newcastle and the Archbishop of Canterbury. Young expressed great thanks and astonishment. Young's years of service in the Church, his achievement as a writer, his long-held position as royal chaplain certainly qualified him for such preferment, and his stature as a poet was to increase immeasurably in the next few years.

As so many writers about Young have repeated each other's adverse charges that he was a place-seeker and overly sedulous in trying to secure preferment—an ambition which they stress as unworthy of a country rector who wrote so effectively in favor of moral values and in support of immortality—it seems important to consider the whole question in the context of the actual preferment system of his time and to examine the records available: to trace in some detail the efforts made directly by his friends and the hopes and encouragement held out to him. From a variety of letters—as his to the Duchess indicating the extent to which he was carrying out her instructions, along with his frequently expressed doubt of success and determination to make no further effort, followed by a new response to her renewed encouragement; a letter to the Duchess from William Murray, a man close to Newcastle, full of encouragement and advice; Young's letters to Newcastle—it becomes evident that the indefatigable seeker of a higher position for him was the Duchess of Portland. And her concern for him arose from friendly affection and admiration and also from her conviction that his being neglected was unfair, undeserved, and incomprehensible.

Full of confidence in the justice of her cause and in the power of the influence of her family and that of her husband, she gave Young not only encouragement but detailed advice on how to proceed. That a man of ability and a sense of mission would naturally have a desire for a more influential position in the Church in no way indicates a mean ambition, but it is interesting to see that it was the Duchess of Portland, the cousin of the Duke of Newcastle, who took the initiative and indeed directed the whole campaign. She knew the people who "counted," and she was aware of what strings to pull—and was willing and eager to pull them.

On August 21, 1742, still from Tunbridge Wells, Young wrote that he had followed her directions, but without visible effect. That he was not overly aggressive in his part of the undertaking is apparent; he had, he wrote, endeavored to make himself known to one recommended nobleman: ". . . I thought I put myself in his way. It was not for me by making the first advance to take his lordship into my patronage; but perhaps I was too shy; I assure your Grace, I'll endeavour to mend for the future." In accordance with the advice of the Duke, he had written to the Archbishop: "It was such a letter, as neither has received, nor expected an answer" (*Bath MSS*, p. 273).

There the matter stood for the better part of a year, but the Duchess's campaign was to gather momentum over several years. Truly, as Young had earlier written about church preferment, "these things are long in coming." In June, 1743, he thanked her for new advice and indicated that he would be grateful for success but would not "repine" at failure; indeed, he even suggested contentment with his present state. In September he again followed her advice and soon after wrote the results: "The day after I saw your Grace I waited on the Archbishop, who told me that my Lord of Portland was very much my friend, but that nothing was to be done without the Duke of Newcastle or Lord Carteret, and presented me with his own good wishes in the handsomest manner; for which I humbly thank my Lord Duke and your Grace. I really believe the Archbishop is my friend"; and, in a jesting tone, he added, "but your Grace knows 'tis dangerous trusting the clergy" (*Bath MSS*, p. 277). On December 14, 1743, he expressed considerable doubt about the whole effort in which she was so much interested, and included an apt comment on the great Duke: "The Duke of Newcastle is our Pope. Ecclesiasticals are under his thumb, and he is as fixed as St. Paul's, by his own weight, in spite of all the revolutions of the little court buildings round about him" (*Bath MSS*, p. 280).

In February, 1744, he thanked her for further advice and expressed willingness to abide by her decisions; and, on May 19, he thanked her for sending him a copy of a letter she had written Newcastle on his behalf. No further word as to the Duchess's progress appears in his letters until February 2, 1745, when he wrote his thanks and amazement at her having enlisted the "kind zeal" of an unnamed, influential man. In June, 1745, she was encouraged by a letter from Mr. Murray, an influential man in Newcastle's department: "I think you conclude too hastily from the D[uke] of N[ewcastle]'s silence. . . . If I was the Doctor, under your protection I would not despair of Windsor, at least not in prose, whatever I did in verse when the night inspired melancholy thoughts" (*Bath MSS*, p. 364).

On the strength of Murray's letter she evidently urged Young to call on Newcastle. On August 21 he wrote her from Tunbridge Wells of his reception: "The Duke of N. received me with great complaisance, ministerially kind, took me by the thumb as cordially, as if he designed it should go for payment in full. In a word, Madam, with great civility—for which I thank your Grace —he—the Duke I mean—had his own pre-engagements, but that he would certainly do what he could; so that if nothing is done, he has kindly prepared me for it" (*Bath MSS*, p. 287). Then Young told her of his conversation at Tunbridge with Mr. Roberts, apparently attached to the official household of Pelham, the half brother of Newcastle. Roberts had reported that he had heard Pelham say that, besides Young's "own good title, the Duchess of Portland was a person, and character, which it was very proper for both him and his brother very much to regard"; and Roberts had added his own advice that, if the Duchess would persist in her effort, she would succeed, that an application should be made for every opening or probable opening, and "that a deanery was as easy to be got as a prebend, as things stand." The Duchess, much encouraged, was certainly willing to persist and to press the matter.

On January 11, 1746, doubtless on her advice, Young wrote to Newcastle to remind him of his existence. On April 6 he wrote the Duchess that he much appreciated all her efforts, and on June 12 he commented on Newcastle's promises: ". . . when I last saw his Grace of N——, he told me he had two or three to provide for before me. Three are now preferred, but perhaps his two or three, like Falstaff's men in buckram, may grow to nine or ten. For what fictions in the extravagance of poesy can exceed the wonderful realities in humble life?" (*Bath MSS*, p. 293). At her advice, he wrote again to Newcastle, reminding him of Young's "very long service and known attachment to his Majesty," and the promises made to him; he pointed out that to a man well along in years "distant expectations are no expectations," and asked for the Duke's favor. But two weeks later, July 17, he repeated his doubts to the Duchess: "Madam, 'tis impossible, 'tis impossible . . ." (*Bath MSS*, p. 294). At this point he seems to have thought the matter ended, but the indefatigable Duchess was evidently still busy behind the scenes.

Early in January, 1747, he wrote to her saying he had followed her instructions and enclosed the letter he had written for her to read and send on to Newcastle. "But whatever success attends your engineering, I shall thank you." On February 3 he again thanked her for all her efforts and declared: "I resign my chimerical expectations." He expressed disapproval of the whole system of preferment, calling it "a sort of curse on the clergy." Yet as she and Mr. Roberts urged him to call on Newcastle again, he consented to do so, in spite of his desire to "call off my thoughts from so dead a scent to other game." Accordingly, on March 3, 1747, he wrote to Newcastle, recalling the Duke's promises and his own long period as royal chaplain. As he suggested, there was indeed something strange in his having been passed over. "It is not only my Loss, but my Reproach and Infamy. . . . What must the world think of me?" [12] And he asked the Duke to reconsider his case. Soon after he wrote further thanks to the Duchess and declared his efforts were over: "I am resolved to stir no further, which is only taking pains to be despised."

But it was apparently not until the next year that the Duchess was ready to admit defeat, as his letter of June 4, 1748, indicates: "I much thank you for your very kind letter, which set my heart at rest from the uneasiness of foolish expectation and suspense. Your Grace's endeavours were not the less kind for being unsuccessful, and to the kindness of a friend our gratitude is due, not to his success" (*Bath MSS*, p. 310).

The decade of the 1740's covered the period of the Duchess of Portland's devoted efforts to secure his preferment, and Young's letters to her show that hers was the initiative in beginning and the persistence in continuing the efforts, and that he had more doubts than hopes of success. In the years remaining to him, there were to be others who were troubled by his lack of preferment; and he naturally enough wondered from time to time why he was the only royal chaplain of long service passed over.

VI *Publications in the 1740's*

Though Young did not discuss his literary activities in his letters during the decade, these years saw the publication of his greatest poetry, the lengthy *Night Thoughts,* many of the ideas and themes of which did find expression in his conversation and letters. In 1741 a very brief poem also appeared, "Epitaph on Lord Aubrey Beauclerk, in Westminster Abbey, 1740," ten lines of heroic couplets, in memory of Lord Aubrey, a grandson of Charles II, who was killed in action at the siege of Cartagena. This officer, one of the most promising in the royal navy, was, of course, a cousin of Lady Betty; but it was his sea service which caught Young's interest. The poem stresses Britain's loss and her mourning for the "dauntless, loyal, virtuous Beauclerk, . . ." "Dying, he bid Britannia's thunders roar;/and Spain still felt him, when he breath'd no more." Young's sentiments are in the spirit of his naval odes.

On May 31, 1742, an advertisement announced the publication of an anonymous poem, "The Complaint," the first of the nine poems comprising the *Night Thoughts.* Two months later a second edition was published with the promise of a second poem before long. Young's friend Benjamin Victor wrote to Young in the summer that he had read it with pleasure: "I found the thoughts quite new and Doctor Young written in large characters in every page." The other poems in the series followed at intervals: *Night II* on November 30 and *Night III* in the middle of December, 1742; *Night IV,* much longer than any of the first three and the only one with a preface, appeared in March, 1743, and was considered to be the last of the series. But in December of 1743 *Night V* was published, followed in March, 1744, by *Night VI,* and in July by *Night VII.* In 1745, *Night VIII* was published in March, and though dated 1745 and usually listed as of that date, *Night IX* was delayed and entered in the Stationers' Register on January 21, 1746.[13]

All nine poems were published anonymously, though the authorship was soon an open secret. During the decade many edi-

tions of each *Night* appeared separately, and in collections of
I–IV, I–VI, VII–IX; and in 1750 the first complete collection appeared of all nine *Nights,* a book destined to be reprinted in more
editions than any other book of the eighteenth century over the
next hundred years. While several of the *Nights* were dedicated to
friends—Arthur Onslow, the Duchess of Portland, the Earl of
Lichfield—it may have been at the Duchess's suggestion that
Young dedicated one to Spencer Compton, the Earl of Wilming-
ton, who temporarily held a key government position at the time;
another to Henry Pelham, Chancellor of the Exchequer; and another to the Duke of Newcastle.

What is now printed as a separate poem entitled *Reflections
on the Public Situation of the Kingdom, 1745,* was first printed
incongruously appended to *Night IX;* but it was speedily de-
tached and given its present title. The "public situation" of 1745
had to do with the national emergency caused by the Jacobite
rising under Bonnie Prince Charlie, the son of the Pretender, who,
having landed in Scotland and rallied great numbers of Scottish
Highlanders to his cause, threatened to seize the throne of Britain.
Young, in this definitely occasional poem, addresses Newcastle,
then serving as Secretary of State, calling on him to put the national crisis ahead of all international problems and to entrust
control only to the ablest leaders.

The poet declares the danger to the nation comes not alone
from the Jacobite threat but even more from national corruption
and irreligion. "Less fear we rugged ruffians of the north,/Than
virtue's well-clad rebels nearer home." The Scots, the Jesuits, and
the French support constitute less of a menace than disunity,
private ambitions, factions, and dishonest counsel. A reawakened
Britain, "the nurse of merchants," "cut from the continent, that
world of slaves," and "dedicated, long, to liberty," will be unshaken if based "on virtue's rock"; for "Armies and fleets alone
ne'er won the day." By way of strengthening his admonition,
Young adds another part, the poet's vision while walking "in troubled thought"—the white cliffs of England in the moonlight with
a message thereon, entitled "The Statesman's Creed," proclaiming
that "As govern'd well or ill, states sink or rise," that state ministers must be upright, that "Religion crowns the statesman and the
man,/Sole source of public and of private peace." His nocturnal

meditations are broken off by the sound of the skylark, symbolic of England's awakening in danger's hour and of a hope for "the first feeble dawn of moral day."

The few references to night and the ending with the lark's song and the dawn tie the poem slightly to the *Night Thoughts,* as do the serious meditations on the essential basis of virtue and religion; but, on the whole, the work represents an entirely different kind of poem and was certainly out of place attached to the greater work. Written in blank verse, it is much more effective in its expression than are his naval odes, to which it is more closely related in its concern with contemporary public matters.

At the end of the decade, Young's belief that a man's worth comes not from rank or wealth but from virtue and honesty found rather touching expression in a brief poem, "Epitaph at Welwyn, 1749," in which he paid tribute to a humble man, probably one of his servants. In lines patterned for a memorial stone, he referred to the virtues of an honest man:

> My friend, James Barker,
> Of perfect piety
> Of lamblike patience

in his hard-working life was a "lesson and reproach to those above him." In many of his letters Young expressed this same respect for the obscure and humble "honest" man.

CHAPTER 6

Chanted Beneath the Glimpses
of the Moon: 1742-45

THE *Night Thoughts* constitutes Young's greatest achievement; and widely read in England, on the Continent, and
in America, it exerted a good deal of influence, was highly admired, and much quoted. While the initial popular reception
came in some measure from the familiarity of much of the subject
matter and the widespread interest in it, the main interest came
from the sense of freshness, newness, and originality and from the
feeling of personal immediacy. On the whole, Young's achievement was not in enunciating new doctrines: he was not an original theologian nor philosopher. Well versed in contemporary
ideas, he was a poet; and he gave expression to those ideas in a
language striking in effective figures and imagery, with a feeling
of warmth and ardor.

Unfortunately, the extreme length of the series of nine poems as
a whole—a drawback even in its own day—presents a formidable
barrier today when "a long poem" is considered "a contradiction
in terms." Furthermore, the whole series is not readily accessible,
selections in anthologies being almost invariably confined to
Night I. But there is no reason to condemn it offhand because it is
not of this generation. Written in the 1740's, it is obviously not in
the fashion of the mid-twentieth century: "It needs no ghost come
from the tomb to tell us this." But many misleading generaliza-
tions, based on failure to read the poem (or poems) and on a
blind acceptance of some of the misconceptions that gained cur-
rency in the late eighteenth century, and others contributed also
by ignorance and prejudice in the nineteenth century, and repeated in reference to Young in the twentieth century, are formidable deterrents to the uninformed modern reader. Consideration
of the actual poem in relation to its background dispels such misconceptions and indicates something of its real nature.

The nine poems were evidently not planned ahead as a series to constitute a whole: one idea suggested another, one *Night* led to the next, and the poet's pleasure in ramification of details and in developing one idea in a variety of ways led to increasing length. Along with a good deal of repetition there is a difference in emphasis and purpose: the first five *Nights* (of 459, 694, 556, 842, and 1068 lines, respectively) are chiefly concerned with moral reflections on life, death, and human nature; and the last four (of 819, 1480, 1417, and 2434 lines, respectively) are almost wholly devoted to Christian apologetics. Even in the first group there is a difference, the so-called elegiac note being more stressed in the second and third *Nights* than in the other two.

Yet the general organization in each is adequate for such a discursive poem, and the discernible connections and cross references contribute to a certain unity of the whole. Each *Night* has a separate title; and, in the characteristic eighteenth-century custom, a descriptive subtitle indicates the major topics. The theme of immortality as an essential in Christianity runs through and unites the whole. Each poem is written in the first person, as a man meditating in the quiet of night on universal themes not necessarily gloomy but serious, reflecting on ideas which had concerned Young in his own experience, reading, observation of life, and thinking, and had found expression to a large extent in his earlier writings, his letters, and his conversation as recorded by his letter-writing friends. The poems are not literal autobiography, and the "persona" does not represent all of Young.

The method of dialogue, used throughout the series, was that of many argumentative prose treatises to clarify points in discussion by presenting conversation between A and B, or their largely uncharacterized equivalents. Young adapts the dialogue form to secure a feeling of personal participation, immediacy, and emotional involvement by having the speaker address arguments and exhortations to the practically silent member of the dialogue, Lorenzo. Slightly characterized as a young man for whom the speaker is much concerned, and who is somewhat chameleon-like in nature, Lorenzo is in the *Nights I–IV* for the most part the "man of pleasure," the "man of the world," the libertine; and in *Nights VI–IX* he is mostly the "atheist" who must be led to realize the existence of God, but sometimes he is inconsistently the "Deist" who accepts natural religion but rejects revealed Christianity. Elements of all of these different characterizations may be found to some extent in most of the *Nights.* To give a more personal effect, Young uses the "characteristical" method he had used so effectively in his *Satires,* and which he uses in Lorenzo, and in several other instances of named characters as well as many unnamed ones designated as "a man I knew" or some such formula. To consider them actual identifiable people is a serious error.

In the *Night Thoughts* Young uses blank verse, at the time a form which seemed new, as heroic couplet had so long dominated the poetic fashion, though the revival of blank verse had been in progress for some years. Many of the rhetorical characteristics of his earlier poetry are apparent here also. Because of the general unfamiliarity with the content of the *Night Thoughts,* a brief summary of each of the separate poems is of value. The title of the first of the series, "The Complaint," became the general title for *Nights I–VIII,* and the final *Night* was entitled "The Consolation," indicating an answer or completion.

I *Summary of Each* Night

In *Night I,* "On Life, Death, and Immortality," the poet, sleepless from grief, is reminded of death by the quiet sleep of the world around. His prayer of invocation for divine aid "to lighten and to cheer" and to "strike wisdom from my soul" suggests the purpose and nature of the poem:

> O lead my mind
> (A mind that fain would wander from its woe),
> Lead it through various scenes of life and death;
> And from each scene, the noblest truths inspire.

The striking of the clock suggests thought of the passing of time and man's waste of it. This thought leads to reflection on the contrasting elements of man's nature as mortal man and immortal soul, with thoughts on the consoling idea that those mourned as dead are living in a larger life, and on the folly of pinning all desires on transitory earthly things. The poet's joy in life had been blasted by the triple loss of friends in a short time: ". . . and thrice my peace was slain;/And thrice, ere thrice yon moon had fill'd her horn" (I, 212–13). But, realizing that he is not alone in such grief and that death is universal, he says that he must not indulge in personal grief; but, aware of troubles of mankind, and deploring the lack of benevolence in the world, he must help others. Addressing Lorenzo, a young man of pleasure, he says that warnings of the impermanence of earthly joys are not unkind; and, referring to the unexpected death of their good friend Philander, who had been unaware of his fatal disease, he warns Lorenzo not to count on the future but to live so as to be always in a state of preparedness for death. The folly of man is that he is always about to live, always about to reform: "He resolves; and re-resolves; then dies the same." The lark's song announces dawn. The poet, striving to "cheer the sullen gloom" of grief, wishes for the genius of Homer, Milton, and Pope; and he says he seeks to supplement Pope's omission of the theme of immortality: "Immortal man I sing."

Night II, "Of Time, Death, and Friendship," begins also with midnight sleeplessness and grief; and, with his fortitude and realization of the universality of human woes, he is determined not to dwell on his personal troubles. The poet, turning to Lorenzo, considers themes suggested by the death of Philander—time, death, friendship, and Philander's "final scene." The theme of time—its value, the folly of wasting time, and the irrevocability of past time—is discussed (from line 25 to line 354) with many effective illustrations. Next, for about one hundred lines, the poet is concerned with "death the leveller"—universal and inevitable—and with the value of reminders of it for man, who is prone to give it little thought and to ignore the way life slips by. Then the poet turns to thoughts of Philander and the theme of friendship, the joy and value of conversation with a friend, the basis of wisdom and happiness in friendship—all shared with Philander, a friend for twenty years. In conclusion he describes Philander's death, "the temple of my theme," which showed his friend, though suddenly faced with death, "undamp'd by doubt, undarken'd by despair," but marked by peace and hope.

Night III, "Narcissa," opens also with nocturnal sleeplessness and grief, and then turns again to the thought of death, here introduced with a specific characteristical illustration (whereas in *Night II* the illustration had been developed at the end). The death of Narcissa, which had occurred shortly after that of Philander and was indeed hastened by his death, differed from his in that she was a young, beautiful, innocent girl, whose death had not been entirely unexpected. Stricken with disease, she had been hurried "with parental haste" to the South, had died there, had been denied a grave because of religious bigotry, and had been buried secretly. An emotion-charged denunciation of such bigotry—not only this Roman Catholic manifestation of the "cursed ungodliness of zeal," but of mankind's general and all-too-common lack of benevolence—indicates that the poet is here dealing with more than one specific situation. The focus on Narcissa's death, on what he calls "my touching tale," comprises only 125 lines of the 536 lines of the whole *Night*, and consequently furnishes a specific illustration of general topics which are considered in *Night III*. The repetitions of life, the staleness of most of the pleasures of the sensual man are contrasted with the more abiding satisfactions of a virtuous man who finds increasing richness pointing to its culmination in the next life. With such thoughts, death loses its dreadfulness, becomes "the great counseller," "the deliverer," "the rewarder," "the crown of life"—not an end but a beginning.

Night IV, "The Christian Triumph; Containing our only Cure for the Fear of Death; and Proper Sentiments of Heart on that Inestimable Blessing," develops more fully—as its greater length permits—some of the same ideas found in the first three *Nights*. Repudiating fears which "black-boding man" may have of physical death, the poet argues that the aged man has no reason to fear death, for it is the deliverer from a life which holds less and less for him, with death of friends and the few remaining pleasures at best "a thrice-told tale." Familiar with the disappointments and reverses of life, sickened by the folly of those aged people who continue to grasp for earthly triumphs, the poet, free from worldly ambition, finds pleasure in retirement. It is guilt alone that makes men fear death. Then, addressing Lorenzo again, he develops the thought that hope comes only through Christ and describes ecstatically the triumph of Christ and the revelation of the Divine in the beauty of the night sky. This leads to the point that the greatest sign of God is seen in his creature, Man, and this to the consideration of the immortal nature of man, whose passions as well as his reason are God-given, and whose soul will be admitted to celestial circles through death. To Lorenzo he points out the supreme value of religion, the sole hope through Christ, the proof of immortality seen in nature, and the necessary proofs from reason to supplement faith.

Night V, "The Relapse," repeats much of the material of the preceding *Nights* but in different words and at greater length. Addressing Lorenzo, the poet agrees that much poetry has been written on unworthy subjects and celebrating vain joys, but he says that his poems are to propound truths of the first importance. He invokes divine aid, finds inspiration in the stars and the quiet of night, feels again his grief from bereavements, but also therein finds wisdom. The themes of this poem are to include man's attitude to death, "the various kinds of grief; the faults of age"; and the nature of death. He will "range the plenteous intellectual field" to gather thoughts to oppose the "moral maladies of man" through reason.

For Lorenzo's benefit he considers the lessons to be learned from Narcissa's early death: the realization of the transitory and uncertain nature of life, the futility of much that is valued in it. Her youth is a reminder to the old of swiftly passing time. Her gaiety stresses the uncertainty of death's approach. This point is further developed by an illustrative allegorical little story of Death as a masquerader, stealing upon people in the midst of their enjoyments. Narcissa's wealth is a reminder that Death the leveler is no respecter of the "fortunate." Additional illustration is given in a series of examples of types of men sacrificing virtue and happiness in the pursuit of wealth. The sad story of Lysander and Aspasia—both blessed in "youth, form, fortune, fame," but dying tragically on the eve of their marriage—adds a further illustration of life's uncertainty and of death's frequent unexpectedness.

Night VI, "The Infidel Reclaimed," has a descriptive subtitle: "Containing the Nature, Proof, and Importance of Immortality. Part I.—Where, among other things, Glory and Riches are particularly considered." It is also provided with a preface indicating the great amount of contemporary dispute about religion and a belief that it may all be reduced to one question: "Is man immortal, or is he not?" Arguments supporting immortality are to be presented, ones "from principles which infidels admit in common with believers."

The poet again begins his poem in midnight meditation by re-calling the loss of a loved one, later referred to as Lucia. He de-scribes the agony of watching her years of illness and the slow approach of death, the eventual "death the deliverer." Then he states his theme: immortality—its nature, proof, importance. As he considers its nature, he describes in enthusiastic, figurative terms the various possibilities of the joys of the immortal soul where there will be no limit to intellectual development, where the whole unlimited field of knowledge will unfold, and where the marvels of creation as a whole will be seen. Proofs of immortality are based on the analogy of nature, the symbolic parallel in the continuous succession of night and day and in the cycle of the seasons. Matter is immortal; can the spirit die? Another "proof" is seen in the marvelous achievements of man in the physical world, in remaking the world for his use—lands reclaimed from the sea, fine arts and noble temples, rivers turned to new courses, dry plains irrigated, canals connecting seas, great navies, and Britain's navy "that awes the world to peace": "Whose footsteps these?—Immortals have been here." Additional proofs are promised in the next *Night*.

Night VII, "Being the Second Part of the Infidel Reclaimed. Containing the Nature, Proof, and Importance of Immortality," has a longer preface, as befits a longer poem, in which the belief in immortality is again seen as the fundamental support of virtue; and doubt of such belief is the basis of the infidel's error. "Some arguments for immortality, new at least to me," are to be devel-oped in the poem in the hope "that an unprejudiced infidel must necessarily receive some advantageous impressions from them."

Beginning the poem with a reference to the recent death of Pope and to the probability of his own death soon, the poet as-serts the truth of immortality and promises proofs from the nature of man, from his feelings. Man's discontent in this world and his hopes suggest a future life, for otherwise he is worse off than the lower animals; for they know nothing of the doubts, fears, fruit-less hopes, regrets, despairs, which embitter man's life. "Admit immortal life," and virtue becomes reasonable and hope is sus-tained. "New, unexpected witnesses" of immortality against the infidel may be found even in man's natural "ambition, pleasure, love of gain," all of which suggest a seeking for the unattainable

here and, if rightly directed, are indications of the great potentialities of his nature: "I feel a grandeur in the passions too."
Without immortality man's search for happiness would be in vain.

In over three hundred lines the poet pictures the horrors of life
if man were denied immortality, the meaninglessness of it, and the
impossibility of thinking that such a world could be the creation
of a God. But, "If man's immortal, there's a God in Heaven." So,
from the nature of man, his passions and powers, his gradually
developing reason, his fear of death; from the nature of hope and
of virtue; from knowledge and love; and from the difficulty of
understanding the complexities of man otherwise, the necessity of
immortality is demonstrated. Realizing that his discussion is becoming rather lengthy and repetitious, the poet sums up his main
points by reference to Philander's death: without immortality, his
life—so admirable and virtuous, so full of pain—would be without meaning. Immortality is essential for man's happiness; and in
this need is seen an argument in its defense.

Nights VI and *VII*, forming a two-part whole, have almost
nothing of the personal elegiac note (the last reference to
Philander being little more than a device to link these poems to
the preceding *Nights*); and both are devoted to one aspect of
Christian apologetics. The "arguments" of the former are largely
from the outward indications of man's nature, and those of the
latter from his inner nature, his feelings, ambitions, passions.
Night VII recalls Young's most outstanding sermon, "The True
Estimate."

Night VIII, "Virtue's Apology; or, The Man of the World Answered. In which are considered, the Love of this Life; the Ambition and Pleasure, with the Wit and Wisdom of the World," continues in 1417 lines the discussion of *Night VII* with an effort to
convince Lorenzo, here a "man of the world," of the vanity of
human life without immortality. The whole poem consists largely
of a wealth of striking metaphors illustrating ideas frequently discussed in the earlier *Nights*. A few illustrative examples will
suffice: The glory of eternity will

> . . . swallow time's ambitions, as the vast
> Leviathan the bubbles vain that ride
> High on the foaming billow. (VIII,35–39)

Here life becomes a "Fantastic chase of shadows hunting shades" (VIII,73). Stunned with noise and choked with dust, men compete "on life's stage, one inch above the grave" (VIII,85–88). The poet bids Lorenzo consider the future for his little son Florello when he is ready to enter "the world," to be received into public life by "men of the world," engrossed in "the fatal stratagems of peace," who behind the mask of politeness conceal their ruthless selfishness. What then will be Florello's education "Through serpentine obliquities of life,/And the dark labyrinth of human hearts?"

Many examples of men of the world are given: "A man I knew, who lived upon a smile. . . ." Two men of the court, trying to outwit each other, are pictured as

. . . two state rooks,
Studious their nests to feather in a trice,
With all the necromantics of their art,
Playing the game of faces on each other,
Making court sweetmeats of their latest gall . . . (VIII,343–51)

The other parts of the triple theme, ambition and pleasure, are shown paradoxically to be the root of vice or virtue, depending on one's conception of life. "Bliss has no being, virtue has no strength,/But from the prospect of immortal life" (VIII,1189–90). Wit is good in its place, but "Sense is our helmet, wit is but the plume." He warns Lorenzo not to let the "cooings of the world allure" him.

Night IX and Last, "The Consolation: containing among things, I. A Moral Survey of the Nocturnal Heavens. II. A Night Address to the Deity," written as a unit in itself but also as the last of the series, is by far the longest, with 2434 lines; and, in many ways, it is by far the most interesting, in spite of some repetition of the earlier material. It opens with an extended epic simile: As when a traveller, weary, rests at evening in a cottage, thinks over his search of what he cannot find, and "cheers himself with song," so the poet, "long-travelled in the ways of men" and "waiting the sweet hour of rest," soothes the pains of age with "a serious song."

The first 539 lines are akin to the earlier *Nights:* the poet invokes the inspiration of Night for "one labour more"; addresses

Lorenzo as a man of the world; and, starting with the *ubi sunt* theme, develops many examples of the transiency of life from the "actors of the last year's scene" and from the relics of the past and reminders of past generations. Thought of the future ending of the world leads to the picture of the Last Day, reminiscent of Young's early poem on the then-popular theme, with the imagery of a mighty drama in a mighty theater. Time itself will end, and eternity begin. Again, as in the other *Nights*, the poet maintains the value of troubles, pains, and evils in the disciplining of man for the immortal life. At this point he announces a change in theme and style: "The consolation cancels the complaint." A second epic simile, akin to that opening the poem, pictures the tired traveller resting on a hilltop, looking back over the country passed through, and thinking of his wished-for home; just so, the poet will pause, look back, and "meditate an end," though that end is "still remote; so fruitfull is my theme." His résumé sums up the preceding *Nights*.

Now comes the change. The theme? "Night's grandeurs," the beauty of the starry heavens, the contemplation of which can expand thought, exalt admiration, arouse awe, and fit "capacities" for "final joy." The poet's invocation for divine inspiration in his "daring song" recalls Milton:

> Thou, who did'st touch the lip of Jesse's son,
> Rapt in sweet contemplation of these fires,
> . . . Teach me by this stupendous scaffolding,
> Creation's golden steps, to climb to thee. (IX,582–92)

He then invites Lorenzo to accompany him on a "tour" of the heavens to "kindle our devotion at the stars."

This "Moral Survey of the Nocturnal Heavens," perhaps the best part of the whole *Night Thoughts*, is primarily devoted to demonstrating proofs of the existence of God from the evidence of nature in order to combat the disbelief of the atheist, represented by Lorenzo. "This prospect vast" is, if rightly considered,

> . . . nature's system of divinity,
> And every student of the night inspires.
> 'Tis elder scripture, writ by God's own hand;
> Scripture authentic, uncorrupt by man. (IX,644–46)

> Devotion! daughter of astronomy!
> An undevout astronomer is mad.
> True; all things speak a God, but in the small,
> Men trace him out; in great, he seizes man—
> Seizes and elevates, and wraps, and fills
> With new inquiries. (IX,771–76)

The immensities of the universe revealed by the new astronomy of Newton suggest mysteries beyond man's comprehension. All the wonders of this world and of human achievements are dwarfed by the wonders of the night's stars. Yet, deplorable to think of, the night, which so plainly evidences the being and powers of God, is used by corrupt men, blind to the divine evidence above them, as a time for vice and crime, as they make "the night still darker by their deeds."

The Greek philosophers had read the truths of natural religion in the stars; Christians, with revealed religion as well, have a double light. In a series of metaphors, he exults in the wonders of the starry firmament, calling it "the noble pasture of the mind"; "the garden of the Deity,/Blossom'd with stars"; "the breastplate of the true High Priest,/Ardent with gems oracular" (IX,1038–45). By contemplation of such great objects, man's mind is made greater and his views enlarged. As he meditates on the "mathematic glories of the skies," he rises to ecstatic wonder and amazement: "Orb above orb ascending without end! . . . What, then, the wondrous space through which they roll? . . . 'Tis comprehension's absolute defeat" (IX,1095–1106). The idea of infinity—infinite space, infinite time—finds enraptured expression:

> How distant some of these nocturnal suns!
> So distant (says the sage) 'twere not absurd
> To doubt, if beams, set out at nature's birth,
> Are yet arrived at this so foreign world,
> Though nothing half so rapid as their flight. (IX,1225–29)

Realizing that many of man's preconceived and treasured ideas may be destroyed by new scientific evidence, he prays for clarity of vision and for an open mind to face reality as revealed by astronomy, to see "Things as they are, unalter'd through the glass of worldly wishes" (IX,1327–30). The great vistas opened to the mind by the development of the telescope fire his imagination: "A thousand worlds? There's room for millions more." At the other extreme, the microscope has revealed the wonders "of fine-spun nature exquisitely small," wonders "though demonstrated, still ill-conceived." Contemplation's nocturnal tour, though visiting other solar systems where "larger suns inhabit higher spheres," and suggesting the possibilities of other inhabited planets, does not reveal the abode of the Deity. God is everywhere. Young, with a grasp of the modern science of his day, expresses his conception of gradual progress in the development of the universe: "Nature delights in progress—in advance/From worse to better" (IX,1959–60). He suggests also a progress of the soul, going through various stages of development in its immortal life.

Perhaps, lest his great emphasis on natural religion should lead the reader to confuse his position with that of the Deists, the poet, combining the religious ecstasy of this vision of the infinite universe of worlds on worlds, of a God far beyond man's comprehension, with the Christian revelation, concludes with an apostrophe to the Trinity (IX,2194–2362). Now he approaches the end of his long poem, *The Consolation,* "for all who read": "Then farewell Night! Of darkness now no more!/Joy breaks, shines, triumphs; 'tis eternal day" (IX,2376–77).

II *Some Misconceptions about the* Night Thoughts

Dangers in interpretating the characteristical illustrations, particularly in the earlier *Nights,* as actual individuals in Young's life have already been indicated. This is what was done by some literal-minded readers in the last half of the eighteenth century. A valuable piece of modern scholarship has thrown light on what seems to have stimulated the identification complex.[1] *Night IV* on its first appearance as a separate poem had been provided with a little preface apparently designed as a kind of apology for, or justification of, its somewhat meandering nature by saying that, "As the occasion of this poem was real, not fictitious, so the method pursued in it was rather imposed by what spontaneously arose in the author's mind on that occasion, than meditated or designed. . . . The reason of it is, that the facts mentioned did naturally pour these moral reflections on the thought of the writer."

The "facts" in *Night IV* are primarily the transitory nature of life and the promise of Christianity (with no development of the elegiac examples of *Nights I–III*). Reference to Young's recovery from serious illness and to his disillusionment with court promises may be considered "real, not fictitious"; and that such facts did "pour" these moral reflections cannot be denied. The main point is to explain the spontaneous and unpremeditated method of organization. It is to be remembered that a somewhat similar expression is found in the Preface to "The True Estimate" that the observations are "by no means drawn from books but the life. . . ." The observations made in the *Night Thoughts* were similarly drawn from Young's life and thought.

In 1750 when Richardson was printing his collected edition of the nine poems, he felt that there should be an introductory preface; and, unable to persuade Young to write one, he suggested that part of the Preface to *Night IV* should be used henceforth as a preface to the whole. Young apparently felt no preface was necessary; but, not much concerned about it, he consented to let Richardson do what he thought advisable. Unfortunately, therefore, when printed as an introductory preface, it was interpreted as applying to the whole; and the conception that all was to be taken as "real and not fictitious" led the literal-minded to attempts at identification of the named characters. Who was Lorenzo? Who was Philander? Who was Narcissa? What three deaths within three months?

With a zest akin to that of the would-be identifiers of Shakespeare's Dark Lady of the Sonnets, attempts were made to fit various actual persons into what seemed given details and, for the most part, with small concern for chronology or common sense— or even lines of the poem. It was really with Narcissa that such identifiers had a field day. The death of Narcissa, with some resemblances to that of Elizabeth Lee to be sure, was taken as a literal account, although there were some difficulties in detail. There grew up a legend of Young as an old man, burying his daughter by stealth, and later mourning among the tombs a triple loss of daughter, friend, and wife, and retiring altogether from social contacts to give himself up to grief and elegiac lamentation. In France the legend of Narcissa flourished especially, mostly with romantic disregard of known facts.[2]

But it was, perhaps, in the identification of Lorenzo that the most extreme limit of absurdity was reached. Though Young had ample opportunity to see and know many a young man who could suggest characteristics for Lorenzo, many identifiers preferred to consider him the poet's son—despite the fact that Frederick was about ten years old when the first *Nights* were written and that it seems a bit hard on him to identify him with the libertine Lorenzo, a widower with a motherless little boy. What price chronology? While there always seem to be people to whom the desire to identify characters is greater than the enjoyment of a creative poem, such an approach is, to say the least, a mistaken and unavailing one in understanding and enjoying the *Night Thoughts.* Fortunately, it has been largely abandoned. Other misconceptions, however, grew out of it and contributed to continuing prejudice.

Insinuations, based on ignorance and prejudice, were made that the contrast between the wholly fictitious pictures of Young as a lachrymose, doddering recluse, bewailing his private griefs, or as a place-seeking man, ambitious of wealth and position, on the one hand, and his themes of eternal values, on the other, indicate a basic insincerity in the poet. And these insinuations were responsible for conceptions which warped some nineteenth-century and even twentieth-century estimates of him.

Unfortunately too, a general misconception that the whole series of the nine poems is "gloomy" has prejudiced many against reading it. Actually, the "melancholy" is on the whole more akin to Milton's "divinest melancholy" or contemplation. The invocation early in *Night I* for divine inspiration makes it evident that the poet is not seeking paths of gloom: "O lead my mind/(A mind that fain would wander *from* its woe). . . ." The poet's optimistic belief in the potentialities of human nature contrasts sharply with the dark scenes of actual life he portrays, scenes no darker than reality, introduced to show the abuse of God-given possibilities. Above all, Young's religious faith is optimistic, with the promise of immortality. Nor indeed does he picture this life as necessarily all unhappy. He warns against expecting unalloyed happiness, and against seeking it in abandonment to the passions and in mere materialism. But, in opposition to gloom, he says, " 'Tis impious in a good man to be sad" (IV,675).

III   *Relation of the* Night Thoughts *to Prose and Poetry on Death*[3]

Though Young's personal bereavements doubtless stimulated to a large extent the writing of the *Night Thoughts,* the whole experience of his life and the great interests of the time must also be taken into account. *Nights I–V* are directly in line with a vast number of prose treatises and poems connected with death. There was an astonishing number of books whose descriptive titles indicate such topics as "consolations against the fear of death," "the four last things," and moral benefits to be learned from bereavements. While a reading of a number of the most outstanding treatises shows a difference in plan and to some extent in specific doctrines, they are all much alike in aim and general scope of material. They are all designed to provide a philosophy wherewith to face death without fear; and, as a basis of such philosophy they emphasize the truth of immortality, which they endeavor to prove by analogy.

This doctrine accepted, the conception of this life as preparation for the next and of death as a transition, as an entrance to, rather than an end of, life is inevitable. Contemplation of death in such a light is hence not a morbid preoccupation but a sensible and practical procedure, leading to a correct evaluation of temporal and eternal things and to a realization of the necessity for constant preparation for entrance to the future life. Consideration of the means of everlasting salvation involves discussion of human nature, the need for regeneration and repentance, and the relation between faith and good works. The troubles and trials of life; the transitory nature of earthly happiness; and the loss of friends, regarded as reminders of death, become really blessings in that they turn men's minds from worldly interests to thoughts of eternity and may therefore be instrumental in securing eternal happiness. The obvious resemblance to the aims and material of these popular treatises readily explains something of the immediate popularity of the earlier *Night Thoughts*.

While, of course, death had been a theme in poetry for centuries, the vast quantity of eighteenth-century poetry concerning death needs to be taken into account. The poems may be divided roughly into two groups: first, those akin to the prose treatises; and, second, those concerned with the physical death of the body. Those in the first group consist of meditations on death, regarded as the leveler, the deliverer, the door to a future life; on the transitory nature of life, the need to be prepared for death, and the value of the wise use of time; and, depending on the length of the poem, of theological reflection on the course of life—all with the idea of dispelling fear of death through Christian faith. It is obviously to this group that the *Night Thoughts* belongs.

Those of the second group, not an entirely new type indeed but numbering many outstanding examples, seem to have been designed to please by horrifying (a type of appeal not new then and not extinct today!), dwelling with macabre details on physical death and the fate of the body in the grave. The most outstanding is probably Robert Blair's *The Grave.* This type of poem came to be accurately enough called "graveyard poetry." An analysis of the elements in a great number of such poems shows the essential characteristics present in greater or less degree: The time should be night; the setting, a place of burial, which, in a poem of any length, should be described. If it is in a building, such as Westminster Abbey, the gloomy deserted interior, with any sound echoing fearfully through the vaults, should be pictured. If in a churchyard, there should be a ruined church nearby with an owl or other bird crying out; yew trees or osiers near the graves; and, apart from the mouldering tombstones, a few skulls or other bones lying around have a good effect. Other details may be added to bring home to the reader the horrors of death. Other less morbid aspects of the theme of death may be included; but, to be classified as "graveyard poetry," a poem should include all or some of these characteristics. To consider the *Night Thoughts* as belonging in this group is one of the most serious misconceptions of Young's masterpiece and indicates a failure to read the poem. None of the characteristic elements are developed; indeed, the poet dismisses them as the "bugbears of a winter's eve" (IV,10–12). Contrary to what some illustrators later chose to depict, the setting is not that of a cemetery.

There is indeed a good deal of significance in the title itself, *Night Thoughts;* that is, thoughts at night. A number of similarly named poems—"Midnight and Daily Thoughts," "A Night Thought," "Midnight Thought (On the Death of Mrs. E. H.)," which consists of reflections on moral preparation for death, "A Thought for Eternity," "Meditations on Death"—use night as the background, free from distractions of the day, and as suitable for serious thought on life and death. These seem to constitute one genre of poems on death; "night piece," the other. A "piece" early in the seventeenth century indicated a painting or picture of a scene, and in literary use a "night piece" came to suggest a fu-

nereal landscape, as in Thomas Parnell's *A Night Piece on Death,*
one of the most outstanding of the "graveyard" poems. Young himself had used the term in his sermon, *A True Estimate:* ". . . a
mind haunted with fear is a hideous *night piece* of storm, preci-
pice, ruins, tombs, and apparitions." But, in his greatest poem,
Young was writing not a "night piece" but "night *thoughts.*"

IV *Theological and Apologetic Background of* Night Thoughts

The religious fervor in the poem—because warmth in religion
in this period has frequently been attributed only to the Methodist
movement, and because the poem was praised by both John Wes-
ley and his brother Charles—has led to a suggestion that Young
may have been influenced by Methodism. Cited in this theory are
such passages insisting on the necessity for emotional intensity in
religion as this example:

> Think you my song too turbulent? too warm?
> . . . O for warmer still!
> Shall Heaven, which gave us ardour, and has shown
> Her own for men so strongly, not disdain
> . . . That prose of piety, a lukewarm praise? (IV,628–45)

Warmth in religion, however, was not peculiar to Methodism.
Lukewarmness had been deplored by Tillotson and others in the
late seventeenth century. Dean Edward Young, the father of the
poet, had regarded it as both unworthy and dangerous: "There
grows more scandal to Religion from Lukewarmness, than from
open Profaneness. . . . There grows more hazard to souls from
Lukewarmness than there does from open Profaneness." [4] Evidences from chronology argue against Wesleyan influence on
Young, for Methodism did not assume its characteristic traits until
1738; and not until field-preaching was started in 1739 did it attract widespread attention. Young's religious views were formu-
lated long before then, and indeed the *Night Thoughts* show no
clear reflection of any ideas peculiarly Methodist. The background of his religious thought belongs to the current of rationalism of outstanding significance in the Anglican Church in the late
seventeenth and eighteenth century.

The developments in rationalism made it inevitable that the rationalistic strain in the Church should become of increasing sig-

nificance. The Roman Catholic questioning of the position of Protestantism, as lacking the basis of an infallible church, spurred Anglican demonstrations of the reasonableness of Christianity and the stressing of the basic substructure of natural religion. By natural religion was meant the knowledge of the existence and attributes of God, the laws of morality, and the truth of immortality which was innate in the human mind or readily learned from nature through reason without any supernatural revelation, and which was as much taught by God as the truths usually considered revealed. The extremes of "enthusiasm" of the numerous fanatical sects of the Commonwealth period and their extravagant claims of personal revelations caused skepticism of any revelation unless checked by reason.

Of the great divines who preached a rational religion in the late seventeenth century none was more popular and influential than John Tillotson. His sermons went through many editions and were widely read in the eighteenth century—and are still very readable today. He considered that the most satisfactory method of establishing the truths of religion was to begin by demonstrating the principles of natural religion and "from that to advance to the proof of Christianity and of the Scriptures, which being once solidly done would soon settle all other things." The term "reason," so frequently used by the rationalistic clergy, did not always mean exactly the same thing; but, for the most part, it seems to mean a faculty, innate but requiring education and development. It differs from the similar divine faculty in degree rather than in kind, serving as an infallible means of judging between good and evil, and is designed to be the guide of the senses and passions; it is a faculty distinguishing men from the lower animals, and serving as the one means of judging the truth.

The salient features of rational orthodoxy include: reason as the basis of faith and the test of revelation; natural religion as the basis of revealed religion; emphasis on good works and morality as essential elements in religion; theories of human nature as not entirely depraved and the passions as intrinsically good; happiness as the motivation of human actions; sociability and benevolence as natural to mankind. The great degree to which reflections of these ideas are readily found throughout *Night Thoughts* indicates that their background is in the current of rational orthodoxy.

Defenses of Christianity were by no means new, but they were particularly numerous at the time. The Boyle lectures on the evidences of Christianity, an annual series of eight sermons established by the will of Robert Boyle, a great scientist himself, were of great interest and influence from 1692 on. In Newton, scientist and theologian, Christianity found an invaluable champion; his great astronomical discoveries afforded new sources for teleological arguments for the apologists, and his statement that more light would be shed on religious truths as more of the secrets of nature were learned gave great promise of continued aid from science. Young was evidently very familiar with much of the apologetic writing of the period.[5] In *Nights VI–VIII* he followed very closely the ideas and expression of purposes of Bishop Gastrell's *Moral Proofs of the Certainty of a Future State* (1725), a book which Young reborrowed from the Duchess of Portland about the time he was writing *Night VI* (*Bath MSS*, p. 156).

But it was chiefly in Newtonian astronomy that Young found inspiration for his defenses of religion. Through it he found new vistas of thought and reality which fascinated him and kindled his imagination. His prayer for release from the limitations of "earth's enclosure" so that his mind might be free to explore the new realms of thought and climb "creation's golden steps" to God indicates the purpose of this "tour through nature's universal orb," the much used "tour" by which apologists for religion sought to prove the existence of God through astronomical details furnished by Newton. The "mathematick glories of the skies" with the myriads of stars moving harmoniously—"Orb above orb ascending without end!/Circle in circle, without end, enclosed!"—provided evidence of God.

Young's knowledge of Newtonian astronomy was definitely up to date in details which he used in giving the old teleological arguments a new life from the new evidences of design afforded in the night skies: In "What order, beauty, motion, distance, size!/Concertion of design! how exquisite!" (IX,1422–23), Young shows a grasp not only of the implications of Newton's discoveries but also of infinity of time and space. From contemplating such ideas he had a feeling of intellectual enlargement and an insatiable desire to know more and more, even if old cherished ideas might be thereby shattered; and he prays for clarity of mind to find and face truth. The great glory of immortality is its promise of ever continuing intellectual development and limitless knowledge, in keeping with the conceptions of infinity afforded by astronomy. In the apologetics of *Night IX* Young gave exultant poetic expression to ideas and theories considered vital in the religious beliefs of his time, and he used those aspects of astronomy which appealed to his imagination and offered possibilities of poetic development. His own intellectual pleasure in such contemplation was something he wished to share also:

> Nor is the profit greater than the joy,
> If human hearts at glorious objects glow,
> And admiration can inspire delight. (IX,733–35)

V *Poetics of* Night Thoughts

In a period when long, discursive poems were in vogue, the *Night Thoughts,* individually and collectively, found ready acceptance. Young's first use of blank verse seemed somewhat new at the time. The chief effect of newness came from the sense of great personal involvement, of emotional intensity; and this effect was achieved not only from discussion in dialogue of great themes of universal concern, illustrated from current life and thought and designed for immediate individual application, but also through the rhetorical style. A variety of devices secures the effect of a speaker tremendously involved in efforts to influence a man for whom he is concerned, through his rapturous contemplation of the beauty and significance of the night skies, his religious optimism, and his realistic appraisal of the evil and shortcomings of mankind. The effect is cumulative—from the piling up of images, of metaphor on metaphor, detail on detail. Often the effect is that of breathless enthusiasm, of an effort to express in words truths which transcend human expression.

It would be virtually impossible to find many pages without examples of such rhetorical devices as apostrophe, exclamation, questions, elaborate repetition. Thus a feeling of urgency is suggested in the transition to a new theme: "What yet remains? Much! much! a mighty debt/To be discharged: these thoughts, O Night! are thine . . ." (IX,539–40). Young is fond of paradox and contradiction: "How poor, how rich, how abject, how august,/ How complicate, how wonderful, is man!" (I,67–68). And of the motions of the stars he exclaims:

> Confusion unconfused! nor less admire
> The tumult untumultuous; all on the wing!
> In motion all, yet what profound repose! (IX,1116–18)

He enjoys such interlocking repetitions as:

> Sweet harmonist! and beautiful as sweet!
> And young as beautiful! and soft as young!
> And gay as soft! and innocent as gay!
> And happy (if aught happy here), as good! (III,81–84)

But in the variety, originality, and abundance of his metaphors one sees Young's most characteristic expression. Abstractions gain concreteness. That natural religion may be learned from the night stars leads to their designation as "the manuscript of heaven," "elder scripture," "material picture of benevolence," "Heaven's golden alphabet," "a radiant choir," all turning the universe to a "temple." A variety of metaphors comments on the unperceived speed of time's passing: ". . . time steals on with downy feet" (V,407); "Folly sings six, while nature points at twelve" (V,635). The striking of the clock is "the knell of my departed hours."

> Time, in advance, behind him hides his wings,
> And seems to creep, decrepit with his age.
> Behold him, when pass'd by; what then is seen,
> But his broad pinions swifter than the winds?
> And all mankind, in contradiction strong,
> Rueful, aghast, cry out on his career. (II,139–44)

A series of metaphors may be introduced in one passage: life in this world is

> . . . the bud of being, the dim dawn,
> The twilight of our day,
> the vestibule . . . (I,122–24)

Much of the imagery of his metaphors reflects the interests and experience of Young's life: his acquaintance with law and assizes; his familiarity with theater and drama; his observations of the court; his abiding interest in ships and the sea.

Above all, Young's style indicates his pleasure in the ramifications of his ideas, of following one suggested by another, and then another and another, expressed this way and then that. His strength is the cumulative effect; but his weakness is prolixity, undue length, and repetition. No poem of the length of the *Night Thoughts* can be without poetic lapses and less inspired moments. But it is not solely from the least good parts that Young's success should be evaluated. Its positive virtues are those that led Johnson to praise it for its "copiousness" and "magnificence of vast extent and endless diversity," and to consider it one of the few poems that gained from being in blank verse.

CHAPTER 7

Final Harvest: 1750-65

B Y 1750 changes in the household at Welwyn had developed. After the marriage of Caroline Lee, Young had secured as housekeeper Mrs. Hallows, the daughter of an old friend, the Reverend Daniel Hallows, who had recently died. Mrs. Hallows, in her late thirties when she came to Welwyn, was capable and efficient; and throughout the rest of Young's life she was of inestimable help to him. While some individuals found her too managing, Young was very grateful to her; and his friends indicated in various letters their satisfaction with her. Late in the summer of 1750 Young spent some time at Winchester at the time of the election for the fellowship at New College, hoping that his son might win it. Unsuccessful, Frederick went to Balliol College, Oxford, in 1751. In 1754 Richardson persuaded Young to stay in London long enough to sit for his portrait by Joseph Highman.

After the long exertions of the composition and the preparation of the many editions of the *Night Thoughts*, Young undertook no major literary work for some years; but new interests arising from his earlier writings appeared. His fame had spread to the Continent, and he was in correspondence with admirers. In 1751 B. V. Tscharner, of the poetry group at Leipzig, spent four days in Welwyn, and in a subsequent letter to a friend he described his visit. He had enjoyed being with "this amiable old man"; he had found Welwyn pleasant and his home well run and agreeable. Young was "gay in his conversation," by no means gloomy, and a living example of the social virtues; they had talked of the *Night Thoughts*.[1] His "amiable old man" was, however, about to begin a busy decade.

I The Brothers

In 1750 Young was approached about the possible production of his old tragedy, *The Brothers*, written by 1724 and withdrawn from rehearsal in 1726. During 1751 and 1752 David Garrick visited Welwyn two or three times about arrangements, and was rather irked at Young's hesitation.[2] Young's eventual consent seems to have been due to his idea that this would be a feasible way to raise a sum of money to donate to the Society for the Propagation of the Gospel, and he hopefully decided on a contribution of a thousand pounds. The possibilities of the old tragedy evidently seemed promising to Garrick, who considered Young's earlier play, *The Revenge,* the best modern play, one of the always successful plays in the company's regular stock. Young must have considered some revision of *The Brothers* for this belated appearance of his play, but to what extent it was changed cannot be determined. The play, as printed after production, still seems essentially the one written for the stage of the early 1720's. Based on a historical episode from Livy, with a few heroic tragedy additions and some possible influence of T. Corneille's play on the same story, *Persée et Demetrius,* it was quite in the vein of his two earlier plays.

Against a background of hostility to the encroaching power of Rome, the plot develops. The two sons of Philip of Macedon, a tyrannical king antagonistic to his subordinate relation to Rome, are both able, ambitious, and skillful in oratory. The highly admirable younger son, Demetrius, a favorite with Rome, is hated by his older brother, the villainous Perseus, who is jealous of his brother's connections with Rome and of the fact that Erixene, a captive Thracian princess, whom they both love, prefers Demetrius. In the tense atmosphere of the court, Perseus and his evil attendant create a series of plots to destroy Demetrius; and, if these fail, they plan to convince the King that one way to test Demetrius' loyalty will be to order him to marry the daughter of the King's favorite: they know he will refuse; and the King, believing him in league with Rome, will order his execution as a traitor.

As these plans are working out, things look black for Demetrius; the King, not knowing whom to believe, has both sons arrested and decrees that both must "plead their cause" before the nobles, judges, and counselors. The "big scene" in which the two princes display their oratorical talents is tense and effective. Demetrius appears innocent, but then comes the test: marry the girl. Demetrius, cornered, is desperate and, planning to find a way out later, agrees. Perseus is disappointed; Demetrius is freed; but Erixene, furious, determines on revenge; and she agrees to the King's urging that she marry Perseus to secure her Thracian throne. Demetrius, having drawn his sword against Perseus, is again arrested; when forged letters make him seem guilty of treachery, he is condemned to death. Erixene, going to see him to enjoy her revenge, finds her love reviving. The truth begins to come out, and Demetrius is freed. All seems promising. But Erixene reveals her unhappy secret: she has been tricked into a secret marriage to Perseus. In despair, she stabs herself; and the stricken Demetrius stabs himself. The King and his faithful counselor pay tribute to him.

Resemblances to the earlier tragedies are evident—the much used themes of revenge, hatred, and jealousy; the ending with a double suicide; the absence of poetic justice. The elevated, artificial style indicates its earlier composition; but that the style was still enjoyed is evidenced by the continuing popularity of *The Revenge*. The numerous directions, "the scene draws," "the scene closes," also show the earlier stage conventions.

At the first meeting of the cast to begin preparations for rehearsal with the author present, according to custom, some argument arose: Young wanted the part of Erixene to be taken by George Ann Bellamy, who had been a friend of Caroline Lee. When she and Garrick disagreed as to her fitness for the role, she offered to give it up; Young objected; Garrick was a bit irked, but agreed to Young's desire. Then she scoffed at a line in the play; Young was annoyed, but she finally mollified him; and later she and Young and Quinn, an actor who had long been a famous Zanga, went out to dinner together.[3] It had been many years since Young had been behind the scenes in this way.

The production was opened on March 3, 1753, with a prologue, written by Dodsley, that sounded very much like those of earlier years with the promise of coming delights. Though the play was originally designed for another type of acting, it was agreed that Garrick as Demetrius and Mossop as Perseus gave a brilliant performance, but George Ann Bellamy was not equal to the part of Erixene. The play ran eight nights and netted Young only four hundred pounds—and he made up the promised thousand pounds for the Society for the Propagation of the Gospel from his own resources.

The play itself received many favorable notices, along with some adverse criticism. Arthur Murphy wrote: "The play attracted crowded audiences . . . the contest between the two brothers produces a vein of oratory not to be matched in any other play. . . . The fable is conducted with art." [4] The contest received much praise. But the epilogue, a traditional part of a dramatic production, caused much discussion. Whether or not Young had provided one, Garrick had David Mallet write an epilogue to provide a gay, witty, suggestive note in contrast to the dark mood of the tragedy. Kitty Clive, who spoke it, gave every innuendo its full value. Murphy, who thought it "without much wit and certainly great indelicacy," felt that in Mallet's last lines he was turning Young's philanthropic plan into a jest:

> A scheme forsooth to benefit the nation
> Some queer odd whim of pious propagation!
> Lord! talk so, *here*—the man must be a widgeon:
> *Drury* may *propagate*—but not religion.

Young had gone to see his play without any knowledge of Mallet's epilogue; and, when he heard it, he was "offended at such coarse obscenity." His indignation is easily understood. Back in 1719 and 1722 he had not objected to the epilogue "written by a friend," in accordance with the then-customary off-color and insinuating wit; but this second epilogue of 1753 seemed to scoff at his objective and to besmirch the whole occasion. Moreover, the taste in epilogues had changed since earlier in the century.[5] Refusing to have Mallet's epilogue printed with his play, Young wrote "an historical epilogue" relating the later events and showing the historical nemesis that overtook Perseus in subsequent years, thereby providing a belated avenging of the wrongs done to Demetrius. This epilogue, not at all essential to the clarity of the denouement of the play, seems designed for readers distressed by the lack of poetic justice. Murphy so admired it, however, that he said *The Brothers* should be revived if only for the sake of Young's epilogue.

II The Centaur Not Fabulous

When the excitement of the production and the printing of *The Brothers* was over, Young turned again to an unfinished "prose piece" mentioned in a letter of 1751, a first version of *The Centaur*. By early 1754 he had a new incentive to complete it. The publication, three years after his death, of Bolingbroke's *Complete Works*, that attacked Christianity, caused a sensation and much writing against his views. Young devoted the summer to his *Centaur* which appeared in 1754 as five letters; these were followed by a sixth shortly after, and the work appeared in definitive form in 1755, with the full title, *The Centaur Not Fabulous. In Six Letters to a Friend, on the Life in Vogue*. While he was writing in 1751, his purpose was doubtless to continue the refutation of Deism which had concerned him since his Oxford disputes with the extreme Deist, Tindal. As contemporary memoirs, letters, and satires indicate, national corruption was increasing with growing wealth; and the immorality of the court life almost surpassed that of the Restoration. The publication of Bolingbroke's *Complete Works* did not so much cause the writing of *The Centaur*, however, as give an immediate incentive for completion and a timeliness of appeal.

In a satirical preface, addressing an unnamed lady, one at whose salon "men of pleasure" gather, Young declares her the most able to put his papers in the proper hands: "The men of *pleasure*, the licentious, and the profligate, are the subject of these letters; and, in such as the fabled Centaur, the *brute runs away with the man:* Therefore I call them *Centaurs*. And further, I call them *Centaurs not Fabulous*, because by their half-human conduct, and character, that enigmatical, and purely ideal figure of the ancients, is not unriddled only but realized." With allegorical modification to fit the modern scene, Young makes the mythological half-man, half-horse Centaur an emblem of the men of pleasure, signifying that "beings of origin truly celestial, may debase their nature, forfeit their character, and sink themselves by licentiousness, into perfect beasts." His letters, designed to contribute to the centaurs' restoration to human beings, are, he says, of "an anti-circean nature." The six letters to a hypothetical friend in the city who, "alarmed at our reigning passion for Pleasure," had urged him to write on that subject, are really discursive prose treatises with the personal immediacy contributed by the letter device.

Letter I, in view of Young's basic belief that, without faith, there can be no real morality, is entitled "On Fidelity." Alluding to Bolingbroke, but without mention of his name, he refers to the "recent and signed instance" of how wit and brilliance can "dazzle common understandings"; and he deplores the waste of Bolingbroke's great talents and his infidelity that has left "proud legacies of its poison to the world." The need for greater spiritual light than that given by unaided reason is shown in the contemporary scene: ". . . an age of . . . pastimes; of riots and distresses; of excessive debts, and excessive expense; of public poverty, and private accumulation; of new sects in religion, and new sallies in sin. . . ." He, "fastened in the country," knows less of the worse ways of the city; but he has seen intemperance and vice in every village and feels that lack of faith is responsible. If his tone in his letters seems too denunciatory, it must be remembered that "no man can strike fire with a feather. . . . It must be a blow of some force, that strikes it out of a heart of flint." Young is certainly closer to the biting Juvenal than to the laughing Horace in his pictures of contemporary society in most of these letters.

The next three letters are each entitled "On Pleasure"; but, while there is some repetition, there is a difference in presentation and emphasis. *Letter II,* considering that "the love of pleasure is the root of every crime," gives a historical illustration of the resultant destruction of kingdoms in the fall of Tyre, with warning parallels for Britain. But, as Young is emphatic in pointing out, excess pleasure is dangerous: "I am not against enjoyment; . . . for without a relish of the good things of life, we cannot be thankful. . . . Enjoy, but enjoy reasonably. . . . To enjoy, is our wisdom, and our duty. . . ." Among the "irreproveable pleasures" is that afforded by gardens: "A garden has ever had the praise and the affection of the wise."

As in other writings, he now deplores the unbecoming levity and pursuit of pleasure in old people; he is appalled at the hectic seeking of diversion by the old who frequent assemblies, who try to prolong the pleasures of youth, and who give themselves up to frivolity. There are three kinds of happiness—that of a man; that of a brute that lacks reason; and that of a wretch, who suppresses or abuses his reason, and seeks only the gratification of his senses —in other words, the Man of Pleasure. Temptation to excess pleasure comes from want of faith. "Thus Infidelity leads to Pleasure; and Pleasure confirms Infidelity; and both together consummate ruin." He ends this letter satirically: "(If this be false) . . .

I exchange my Bible for Bolingbroke; and prepare for the Ball: for N. B. I am but fourscore."

In *Letter III*, by way of variety, Young presents the picture of a man of virtue to illustrate his point by contrast. Eusebius, a man of faith and moderation, finds rational pleasure in some of the things in which the Man of Pleasure centers all his desires. He has taste, spirit, and wealth; he is young, gay, and rich; and he is not shocked at masquerades nor cards. But he avoids excess, and he considers his wealth entrusted to him for doing good, for helping others through "bounty and patronage." His pleasures, rational and moderate, are based on the social virtues of benevolence and unselfishness and on the spiritual virtues of faith. In contrast, the selfishness of the Man of Pleasure and his excesses give him no lasting happiness. This fact is illustrated through the dying anguish of a young man whose unkindness and selfishness have brought misery to his family.

In *Letter IV*, Young begins with reassurance to his pessimistic friend that there is hope that times may improve, and he continues with the contrast of the Man of Pleasure and the good man by suggesting the kind of prayer that each might utter; for prayer is "the desire of our hearts." The profligate's prayer may be seen from a few pleas: "Thou great fountain of Pleasure! Give me my heaven on earth. . . . Let my honour too shine before men. . . . Give my lusts a long and prosperous reign over me; and let not religion approach to harm me. . . ." In contrast, the very lengthy prayer (about fourteen pages!), divided into four parts and entitled "devout Thoughts of a Retired Penitent," gives the impassioned cry of a penitent soul that is in extreme contrast to the rest of the letter. Turning to his hypothetical friend, Young points out that they are old and that all too often religious sensitivity becomes dulled in the aged. Prayer is the means to preserve it. "Devotion . . . is the golden chain of union between heaven and earth: keeps open the blessed communication."

Letter V, "Life's Review. The General Cause of Security in Sin. Thoughts for Age," proposes a variety of topics in a way characteristic of various other writings of Young. He recommends a retrospective look over a man's life to draw some moral or a little wisdom for the future, and he suggests many things which may be regretted on such a backward view: ". . . fruitless friendships, unmanly flatteries . . . opportunities lost . . . blessings neglected and trifles admired. . . ." Then he points out: "What on retrospect appears to be the capital weakness of man, is that strange ascendant which his wishes have over his understanding. It is this that makes the Centaur."

Would one want to live his life again, Young asks in metaphoric terms of life as a comedy played by strolling players: "Would'st thou repeat thy part in the comedy? . . . Would'st thou be re-jumbled in this rough Thespian cart, dragged on by those two skeletons, half starved *hope* and panting *expectation,* through bad roads, now worse and worse, and thy fellow-strollers in a constant conspiracy against both thy pay and thy applause. . . . Thou would'st not." Man feels secure in sin because he presumes on God's mercy: "God is indeed love: but shall man therefore be a monster?" This letter too ends with a comment on the proper behavior of the old: many old men are still scheming for more riches and are "still milking the world after it is dry." Age should be a period for meditation and for looking forward to a new life. To see "grey hairs playing the fool" shocks common sense.

In *Letter VI,* "The Dignity of Man," Young presents first the potentialities of human nature, concerning which he had often written; and then, in turning to the striking contrast of the actualities of the Centaurs, he changes in prose style and tone to heighten the contrast. On the "enchanted ground" of the Centaurs he begins his exorcism "to free them from the evil enchantments under which they live . . .": "May . . . these gorgons, furies, harpies . . . syrens, centaur-making syrens! paid or unpaid, keeping or kept . . . may they cease from this hour, to sing or dance, . . . please or plague, pray or swear, our British, unbritish youth, manhood, and age, out of their senses, health, estates, reputation, human nature, and hopes of heaven!"

He pictures the restoration of some: "One burns his Bolingbroke; another an indecent song." Some pay their bills; some give their ill-gotten gambling winnings to charity. Some begin a gradual change, sloughing off a mane, or tail, or other part of the Centaur's outside. "But the process is gradual; nature advances, never leaps. . . . They became not Centaurs all at once." Some, restored, attack Bolingbroke-castle, "a castle built out of the various ruins of the many demolished forts of infidelity, pompously put together. . . ."

Dropping the allegorical and mythical figure, Young returns to consideration of the dignity of man as a more fitting concluding theme. Here a characteristic difficulty presents itself: so many related ideas occur to him that he cannot "get loose from this ever-teeming, all important, and inexhaustible theme." He must reiterate much he has said of immortality, of the necessity of faith, of the unfortunate licentiousness of the day; and with difficulty he draws to an end.

The various editions of this attack on the immoralities of the day suggest that there was some demand for it: two editions in 1755; others in 1765, 1783, and 1786 in separate editions and in the collected editions of his works. But it would be impossible to prove the degree of success in effecting reform, though Thomas maintained that it had a great effect on the court of George II (*Le Poète Edward Young*, p. 188)—a suggestion not easily believed. The conception of human nature, its potentialities, its weaknesses, its strength, and the necessity of a basis in faith all belong to Young's whole belief. The "gloom" arises only from the realization of the evils of the world, especially of the immoralities and dehumanization of the court and "the men of pleasure." In his belief in the possibility of the restoration of the Centaurs there is optimism. (Swift had offered no such possibility for his Yahoos.) The sincerity and social concern manifested in *The Centaur Not Fabulous* is evident. The volume is, as Young himself suggested, overlong and tends too much to repetition; but it is far more interesting than one might expect. Unfortunately, much of it is applicable today. Theological differences, or perhaps differences in theological language, separate it, however, from the twentieth century; but many of the basic conceptions and too many of the ways of the Centaurs remain.

III *A Question of Preferment*

After the completion of *The Centaur*, Young was busy with a new collected edition of his works which was published in 1757 in four volumes "corrected by himself." Late in the summer of 1757 serious illness interrupted his work, and he went to Bath to regain his health. In the spring of 1758 he suddenly decided to take his regular royal chaplain's turn in preaching before the king, although for some years he had furnished a substitute. The sermon, a very short one, was prepared for printing; and the dedication to the King underwent so much revision that finally no reference remained to his long unrewarded chaplaincy except the signature as "your ancient servant." The sermon was published with the title "An Argument drawn from the Circumstances of Christ's Death, for the Truth of Religion."

Young sent a copy of it to the new Archbishop of Canterbury, Thomas Secker, as a suitable gesture from a royal chaplain. In a letter of thanks, the Archbishop said that he had long wondered that "more suitable notice of your great merit hath not been taken by persons in power; but how to remedy the omission I know not." [6] Young was led to wonder again just why he was the only royal chaplain who had not been preferred in all these years, and he wrote to the Duchess of Portland and to Newcastle asking to know what the real reason was, in spite of all the promises and the support of two archbishops and others. He received no answer to his question. These letters of his were not requests for preferment, but only the expression of a deep desire to know why he had received none. It must be remembered that his being "passed over" would be construed by some as a reproach, an indication of some unworthiness or of some positive ill-doing. Some of his friends were constantly feeling that his worth should be recognized, and his foreign friends seemed to expect him to become a bishop or an archbishop.

It may be that, in spite of his consistent Whig political allegiance, connections with individuals of the wrong political group had had much to do with it. It may also have been that Newcastle's desire to profit politically by judicious church appointments and his preference to appoint an individual whose vacated position could be used for another applicant ruled Young out. His benefice at Welwyn, in the gift of All Souls College, could not be used by Newcastle in an ecclesiastical "swop." Young had nothing "to trade in," nor was he of great enough political significance to the powerful Duke. Young differed from hundreds in the competitive scene only in his eminence as a writer.

Late in the same year, 1758, the Duke and Duchess of Portland offered him a benefice in their "gift"; but, as it could not be held with Welwyn, he asked that it be given to his son, if possible: "My son, Madam, is a student at Balliol College in Oxford; he is between twenty-five and twenty-six years of age; I left the choice of his way of life to himself; he chose Divinity; his tutor writes me word that he makes laudable progress in it, and will take orders very soon." [7] Though the benefice was not given to Frederick, Young's letter is important as one of the very few records about his son and as showing Young's affectionate care for him.

IV   Conjectures on Original Composition

Conjectures on Original Composition in a Letter to the Author of *Sir Charles Grandison,* published in May, 1759, is an astonishing production for a man of seventy-six. Its exuberant, forward-looking attitude, its repudiation of dependence on the past, its stress on originality and individual self-confidence, its indignation at pettiness and servility to rules, its ranking Shakespeare with the greatest of the Greek dramatists, its hope for future writers equalling or surpassing the great writers of the past—all suggest a youthful vigor of mind and imagination unusual at his age. It would be an incredible production if it indicated entirely new convictions on his part. While it shows the final development of his views, it does not contradict his past writings. It was no impromptu production, but the result of long deliberation and careful revision.

A glance back over his whole literary career recalls his interest in questions of literary criticism—his awareness and evaluation of theories and practice of the drama, qualities and characteristics of the ode, the nature of satire. His letters, especially those to Tickell, show a lively interest in contemporary literature. But most significant, as pointing forward to the *Conjectures,* is the value he always put on originality; and his characteristic tendency to point out that, whatever he is doing, is "new," or "new at least to me." As far back as 1728 in his *Discourse on Ode,* he had maintained the superiority of "originals" over "imitations." He evidently mulled over such ideas for many years. What then led him to the *Conjectures* so late in life?

When in 1756 Young was honored by Joseph Warton's dedication to him of the first part of his *Essay on Pope,* he seems to have been so struck with some comments in that dedication that he was led to attempt to crystallize his own views by writing. Warton's ideas that seem to have started him concerned the distinction between a man of wit, a man of sense, and a true poet; his point that one essential of a true poet is "a creative and glowing imagination"; and the comment that the sublime and the pathetic are the "two chief nerves of all genuine poetry." The *Conjectures* as

finally published owes much of its zest, not only to the championing of individual independence, but also to the vigor and the metaphoric imagery of his expression.

As the second part of the title indicates, Young uses the device
of a letter to a friend to secure a personal quality lacking in a
formal essay or treatise, and to permit a freer organization. His
opening paragraph, disarmingly apologizing for occupying his old
age with "the pastime here sent you," not only suggests that the
work is "miscellaneous in its nature" and free from usual rules in
its development, but also shows evidence of careful organization
in the provision for the last part of the letter: "I have endeavoured
to make some amends, by digressing into subjects more important, and more suitable to my season of life. A serious thought
standing single among many of lighter nature, will sometimes
strike the careless wanderer after amusement only, with useful
awe: as monumental marbles scattered in a wide pleasure garden.
. . . To such a monument I may conduct you. . . ." He re-
minds the friend whom he is addressing that another "friend" had
asked for "our sentiments on *Original* and *Moral* Composition,"
and he states that he will begin with original composition and
later will consider serious drama and moral composition.

Before turning to his main theme, which appeals to him as "an
original subject to me, who have seen nothing hitherto written on
it," he considers the value in general of composition. Though some
have said that too much is being written, he affirms that, provided
it is based on "sound Understanding and the Public Good," "the
more composition the better." It provides a recreation, a refuge,
and a source of delight: "It opens a back-door out of the bustle of
this busy, and idle world, into a delicious garden of moral and
intellectual fruits and flowers; the key of which is denied the rest
of mankind. When stung with idle anxieties, or teased with fruit-
less impertinence, or yawning over insipid diversions, then we
perceive the blessings of a letter'd recess. . . ." Composition can
afford a refuge from the rush of the city and a protection from the
"sloth and sensuality" of the country. Above all, it can relieve "the
languors of old age," and give honorable occupation to him
"whose unsteady pen vibrates to the last in the cause of religion,
of virtue, or learning."

Young then turns to the main theme and, in a metaphor of gardens, plants, and growing things, which is a dominant metaphor

throughout, he introduces his major terms: "The mind of a man of genius is a fertile and pleasant field . . . it enjoys a perpetual spring. Of that spring, *Originals* are the fairest flowers: *Imitations* are of quicker growth, but fainter bloom." He indicates that he will use the term "Originals" for those who imitate nature, and "Imitations" for those who imitate authors. The first is always superior to the second: "An *Original* may be said to be of a vegetable nature; it rises spontaneously from the root of genius; it *grows*, it is not made." Since thoughts, as well as words, get worn with use, writers should think for themselves: "We may as well grow good by another's virtue, or fat by another's food, as famous by another's thought."

Why is it, he asks, that there are so few originals? It is largely because the writings of the past overawe writers of the present: "They *engross* our attention, . . . ; they *prejudice* our judgment in favour of their abilities . . . ; and they *intimidate* us with the splendor of their renown." Although writers of the past are of great importance to those of the present, they should be admired, not copied. This distinction between copying and imitating other writers leads him to a differentiation between the relative value of genius and learning. Learning is "a great lover of rules"; genius, with less interest in rules, "has ever been supposed to partake of something divine," and surpasses learning, great though its worth is.

A supreme example of a modern genius is Shakespeare. There are two kinds of genius: first, the "adult," which "comes out of nature's hand" fully grown; and second, the "infantine," which must be nursed and educated by learning, and which is sometimes in danger of being misled or smothered. Genius, Young feels, is less rare than is usually believed; and the great danger to genius comes from imitation. In the first place, imitation prevents progress in "the liberal and politer arts." Next, it encourages conformity: "Born Originals, how comes it to pass that we die Copies? That meddling ape Imitation . . . destroys all mental individuality." Furthermore, imitation "makes us think little"; and it leads to the production of big books with little value.

Questioning why the moderns, equal in ability to the ancients, should fall short in achievement, Young suggests that the ancients had a more favorable intellectual climate: they had great patrons who provided "the marvelous sunshine" which encouraged the "crop" of the "fruits of genius." The trouble with the moderns is that they do not realize the potential dimensions of the human mind. To encourage original composition, Young gives two rules: (1) *Know thyself;* and (2) *Reverence thyself:* "Therefore . . . learn the depth, extent, bias, and full fort of thy mind; . . . excite and cherish every spark of intellectual light and heat . . . let not great examples, or authorities, browbeat thy reason into too great a diffidence of thyself." This enthusiastic counsel, developed at greater length, distinguishes Young from many critics of the past who had endeavored to restrain the would-be writer, bidding him keep in mind his limitations.

Young continues with a discussion of the difference between "the well-accomplished scholar, and the divinely-inspired enthusiast." Hence comes the inferiority of translations. More significant than his consideration of the limitations of Pope and Swift is his enthusiastic and optimistic idea of the progress of poetry: ". . . the day may come, when the moderns may proudly look back . . . reputing *Homer* and *Demosthenes,* as the dawn of divine genius. . . ." Parallels in other fields of knowledge suggest such progress: ". . . and these are new food to the genius of a polite writer; these are as the root, and composition, as the flower, and as the root spreads, and thrives, shall the flower fail?" There is hope for new developments in original writing, especially in England, which has already had great Originals—Bacon, Boyle, Newton, Shakespeare, Milton. The moral obligation of writers is to follow their example as Originals. The "gift of talents implies an injunction of their use." He alludes to the original composition of the novels of Richardson, who converted fiction to moral ends.

As he celebrates the supreme achievement of Shakespeare, an Original and the equal of the Greek dramatists, he embarks on the topic of serious drama; and, in the course of his discussion, he indicates the flaw in several of the outstanding English dramatists: Ben Jonson was an imitator, weighed down by learning; Dryden's tragedies lacked pathos, and were further ruined by rhyme; Addison's *Cato* suffered from the same lack of pathos: "His beauties sparkle, but do not warm. . . ." In coming to Addison's prose, to which Young rightly feels his lasting reputation will be due, he touches on moral composition, and goes quickly on to the serious digression mentioned at the beginning—the story about Addison's calling his stepson to his deathbed and saying, "See in what peace a Christian can die." All Addison's "compositions are but the noble preface; the grand work is his death." Evidently aware of the degree to which this final part is unrelated to the main topic, Young comments: "This you will think a long digression" (a comment none will gainsay). This is the "monumental marble" designed to promote serious thought.

With definite allusion to an idea expressed by Addison in the *Spectator* (No. 349) that "the end of a man's life is often compared to the winding up of a well written play," Young, now referring to Addison's death, bids us "regard the person departing as an actor of a part. . . . This was a Roscius on the stage of life; his exit how great? Ye lovers of virtue! *plaudite*." Young adds in a postscript that further discussion of Addison as an Original will be given "in my next."

Modern scholarship has shed interesting light on the postscript and on how Young came to include the unrelated last part concerning Addison's death.[8] Young had apparently planned to write two essays, one on original and one on moral composition; and the story of Addison's death was to be the high spot of the second story. Richardson, enthusiastic about the hitherto unknown anecdote, persuaded him to move it to the first paper and made some suggestions about telescoping it into its new setting. Though Young struggled with the second paper, he did not complete it; and the reference in the postscript was left dangling. Young had great doubt about the advisability of the changed position of the anecdote, and after publication Richardson too felt it a mistake— as did many others (Richardson, *Correspondence*, II,54).

The immediate reception of the *Conjectures* was good.[9] Richardson wrote to Young that such people as Onslow, Johnson, Warburton, and Allen of Bath had expressed pleasure in it. Unfortunately, the papers giving Johnson's more detailed opinions, which Richardson said he had sent, never reached Young. Various favorable comments appeared in periodicals. The *Monthly Review*, though disliking the style, praised Young as having the "qualities of a genius of the first rank" and considered his observations as "new, striking, and just." Many of the readers were struck with the amazing youthfulness shown in the writing of a man of Young's advanced years. His friend Mrs. Delany declared it "is written with the spirit of twenty-five rather than four score years of age."

The meeting of Young and Johnson at Richardson's house which Johnson spoke of to Boswell many years later is unfortunately not discussed in extant letters of the time it took place, somewhere between January and May, 1759. Boswell recorded that Johnson said he was surprised that Young considered as novelties what he thought very common thoughts.[10] Just which points Johnson had in mind is not clear. Certainly Young had himself much earlier expressed many of the same ideas, and there was a vast amount of discussion of related points during the century.

Though both Young and Richardson seemed somewhat interested in further revisions, there were only a few minor verbal changes in the second edition, later in the same year, 1759. No other editions appeared during Young's life. The *Conjectures* had a much greater reception and exerted a much greater influence in Germany: within two years of its publication, two translations into German appeared; and these have been credited with playing a large part in the development of the "storm and stress" movement. Though the *Conjectures* was included in the various *Complete Works* from 1773 on, no separate, new edition was published in England until the end of the second decade of the twentieth century. The edition by Edith Morley of 1918 did a good deal to revive interest in it, and it has come to be considered an influence in the Romantic movement. It is now included in various anthologies of literary criticism, as a whole or in part; and *Conjectures* is therefore more accessible than most of his other writings.

V Resignation

In the *Conjectures* Young had suggested that composition could serve as a defense against the languors of old age, and in 1761 he had an opportunity to combine this value with that of consolation. Mrs. Montagu induced him to write a poem for her friend, Mrs. Boscawen, who, very depressed at the death of her husband, Admiral Boscawen, had found some comfort in reading the *Night Thoughts. Resignation,* written without thought of publication, was printed in a private edition by September, 1761. It was so well received by friends that Young was led to publish it in 1762.

As the preliminary letter printed in the private edition indicates, he did not confine himself to the theme of the title but touched on many topics: ". . . the Vanity of this Life and the Value of the Next; Patience; Prayer, Death; the great Goodness of

the Deity, etc." The poem has no very firm structural organization; one idea leads to another with much amplification. The
poem is long and proceeds at a leisurely pace. The stanzaic pattern, quatrains of the ballad type, is unfortunately not entirely
suited to the topics; but it is interesting that Young should experiment at this late date with a form he had not used before.

After some stanzas of apology for the weakness of old age—his
near-blindness and his trembling hand—the poet settles on his
theme, which he characteristically finds to be new: "O Resignation! yet unsung,/Untouched by former strains. . . ." With the
thirty-second quatrain, the argument proper begins: it is *thought*
that provides answers, that "plucks the frightful mask from ills,"
and shows that they may be ultimate blessings: "And ev'ry sorrow
cuts a string,/And urges us to rise." This idea, expressed so often
before and so much more effectively, is developed at length.
Young himself had recently received a new blow in the death of
his great friend, Samuel Richardson, and he pays tribute to him
for his help in the past and praises the great insight into life in his
novels. He urges a firm stand against giving way to undue grief, a
contemplation of enduring values, and a realization that "Joy is
our duty, glory, health."

The second part of the poem focuses on the value of religion,
the need to consider the real significance of death, and the promise of a future life. He censures the old who forget their age and
are concerned with the ephemeral pleasures of youth. His own
theme is gratitude for the goodness of God to man. In lines recalling the imagery of the *Night Thoughts* (the source, not the style),
he points to the "ample manuscript of the sun, and moon, and
stars" where truth may be read; and he reflects that over his whole
life God has been "propitious to my peace." Self-knowledge is the
mother of resignation: in his own mind, man will find the evidence of God; in contemplating the potentialities of man, his
place in the vast cosmos, and his dependence on God, he will find
peace and resignation.

Resignation is almost a kaleidoscope of fragments of thought
and imagery familiar from his earlier writing, but expressed in unsuitable rhythm and rhyme, in an overlong, meandering form. It
seems an immeasurable distance from the exuberant youthful
spirit of the *Conjectures,* published only two years earlier. But it
represents a heroic struggle of an old, sick, almost blind man

against the ravages of age. It is his final expression of his optimistic faith rather than an achievement of poetry. Furthermore, it seems to have been a source of comfort to many people.

VI *Last Years*

During the period of composition of *Resignation* Young was also busy with the "correction" of another collected edition of his works which was published in 1767 in four volumes, the last edition "corrected" by him. The first volume included an "advertisment of the author" as a sort of foreword: "I think the following pieces in four volumes to be the most excusable of all that I have written; and I wish less apology was needful for these. As there is no recalling what is got abroad, the pieces here republished, I have revised and corrected; and rendered them as pardonable, as it was in my power to do." Understandably, to come within the scope of the four volumes, some less significant pieces were omitted. A fifth volume in 1773 contained some of his major prose, and a sixth in 1778 contained everything else that could be found on the basis that "the slightest performances of a great master are always esteemed."

Young's last few years were brightened by letters from friends of many years in England and by a growing correspondence with admirers on the Continent. Dr. Johann Arnold Ebert's translation of the *Night Thoughts* into German pleased him. By 1759 his parish work was lightened by his securing the assistance of Mr. John Jones as curate, an advantage later outweighed by the damage done by gossip and by the publication of the malicious letters of this warped, frustrated, disappointed man which contributed to misinformation about Young.[11] More reliable information comes from the letters of Young's many friends and of his letters to them. Under the capable management of Mrs. Hallows, Young's Welwyn home remained a center of hospitality.

In March, 1759, his friend Joseph Spence visited him for several days; and the two went over Spence's anecdotes to check them for accuracy. Young indignantly declared false the story of his having been given a human skull as a candle holder by Wharton, and also rejected the anecdote of having received a large sum of money from Wharton for the *Satires*. It is very unfortunate that Spence corrected only one of his two manuscript copies of his anecdotes and that the uncorrected one found its way into print and became the source of damaging gossip which still appears in writing about Young.[12] While Spence may have paid a second visit to Welwyn early in 1765, no accounts of it are to be found.[13]

In 1760 Mrs. Montagu visited Young on September 19, and in a subsequent letter to her husband she praised Young's conversation: "His conversation has always something in it very delightful; in the first place it is animated by the warmest benevolence, then his imagination soars above the material world . . ." (*Correspondence*, II,199). The next year on April 9 he wrote of his delight at a projected visit from her and Mrs. Carter. After Richardson's death, July 4, 1761, knowing how deeply grieved Young would be, Mrs. Montagu invited him to come to Tunbridge Wells as her guest; but he was unable to accept. The next year, the death of his friend from early years, Dodington, now Baron Melcombe of Melcombe Regis, must have saddened him.

Though he was outliving many old friends, new ones came into his life. His friendship with George Keate, a young man with literary tastes, began in 1760; and Keate's frequent letters, his annual gifts of his latest books, and a visit to Welwyn all brought fresh interest. Young's letters to Keate[14] show his pleasure in exchanging literary opinions and in hearing of goings-on in the world of writing. Though his sight was, by late 1762, so poor that he could no longer read nor write readily, he continued his correspondence, with Mrs. Hallows as amanuensis. In March, 1764, his comments to Keate on spring publications are quite in the tone of his earlier writing: "Every spring produces Daisy authors, which true taste treads underfoot, but it is well if genius, like the aloes, vouchsafes to blossom once in fifty years." His correspondence with the Duchess of Portland continued until shortly before his death, and his pleasure in welcoming visitors and his interest in people and contemporary affairs remained unabated. One visitor, hoping to hear him talk about the days of Queen Anne, was somewhat disappointed to find the aged poet more interested in hearing about affairs in the time of George III (Boswell, *Life of Johnson*. Oxford, 1935–50, IV, 59).

On the accession of King George III, Young had received a blow to his old man's pride: in revising the list of royal chaplains, the young King had—rather cruelly—removed Young's name. Before long, however, he was appointed by the King (Young thought the Duchess of Portland's efforts responsible) to the almost purely honorary position of chaplain to the Princess Dowager of Wales, the widow of Prince Frederick.

Young's will of 1760,[15] with a codicil of 1764, is valuable as indicating the number of his remaining friends to whom he left memorial rings in the custom of the day. He left larger bequests to Mrs. Hallows, Mr. Jones, his "dear nephew Richard Harris," and others; and the residue of his substantial estate went to his son. A most regrettable feature of the will was the provision for the burning of all his papers, except his account books; for, as his correspondence was large, a great many letters were thereby lost which would have been of great value in later years.

The will of 1760—as well as each of the few records left concerning Frederick—indicates Young's devotion to his son; and not until 1761 can any indication of any estrangement or difficulty be documented. In a letter of June 9, Mrs. Carter asked Mrs. Montagu: "Have you proceeded at all in a design so truly worthy of you, as attempting to make peace between Dr. Y——— and his son?" (Shelley, p. 111). Unfortunately, Mrs. Montagu's reply—if any—is not available. About a year later, in July, 1762, in one of his characteristic letters, hinting at mysterious goings-on at Welwyn, Mr. Jones wrote about Young: "There is thought to be an irremoveable obstruction to his happiness within his walls, as well as another without them; but the former is the more powerful and like to continue so" (*Gentlemen's Magazine*, LII, 283–84).

The first "obstruction" evidently referred to Mrs. Hallows, whom Jones cordially disliked and frequently maligned; the second may be a reference to Frederick, but this cannot be substantiated. Anyone who has read the vituperative descriptions of the many people Jones hated, and in the writing of which he seemed to vent much of his resentment and worry, must hesitate to accept without reservation anything he said. But that there was some difficulty between Young and his son seems indicated. Frederick may well have found Balliol College with his friends, Ditchley with his maternal relatives, and Chiddingfold with his paternal relatives more congenial than Welwyn with his seventy-nine-year-old father and his friends. Various persons have concocted theories. Actually, we have no adequate knowledge even of the nature nor the extent of the difficulty, and the matter has received too much notoriety from the malicious gossip of Young's curate. When in the spring of 1765 Young became seriously ill, Mrs. Hallows sent for Frederick; and he came immediately. Young, suffering great pain though under opiates, was too ill to talk with him or see him; but on his deathbed he blessed him. Young died on Good Friday, April 5, 1765, some weeks before his eighty-second birthday, having lived from the closing years of the reign of Charles II to the early years of George III.

CHAPTER 8

Two Hundred Years Later

WIDELY read and admired during Young's lifetime, many of his writings retained their appeal well into the next century. On the Continent, where the *Night Thoughts* had found an immediate admirer in Klopstock, had been admired by the young Goethe, and had proved a comfort to Robespierre and Danton, its popularity continued, lingering on into the twentieth century in devout circles.[1] In England the last complete collection of his works was published in 1854, though selections appeared in various nineteenth-century books in England and America. His popularity gradually died away until today even his greatest poem is little known, and misleading and misinformed comments remain in print.

Through this general study of Young's life and of what he actually wrote, in relation to the period in which he lived, it is possible to estimate his achievement more justly than has always been done. Some understanding of the all-pervasive influence of the political situation in an era of political upheavals and crises and a realization of the effects of the intrenched system of patronage and the unfortunate system of church preferment shed light on the unavoidable hazards in the career of any clergyman and writer—including Young. Conventions of language—the accepted forms of address to monarchs and aristocrats, the customary terms in adulatory verse, even the formality of manners and language in polite circles—form part of the situation of the period rather than peculiarities of an individual. With a realization of what must be accepted as social customs different from those of another time and not as unfortunate personal characteristics, it becomes possible to get a truer picture of Young.

With the exposure of misconceptions derived from prejudice and ignorance, the false and warped image of Young is corrected. The evidence of his own writing, of his letters, of the events of his life, and the records of his friends and of others who knew him provides a very different picture: he emerges as a man with a sense of humor and a taste for satire, as clever, witty, accomplished; as a good conversationalist, at home in many kinds of situations; as a man with many devoted friends and an interest in people; as a man of wide interests and depth of thought. His life at Welwyn was not one of great retirement.

Read in proper perspective, his writings show an interesting consistency and development. The constant expression of his concern with the basic and essential values of religious faith shows his growing and developing sense of the mystery of ultimate reality. His interest in the theories and conventions of literary expression and the value of originality is seen from his earliest poem to his last great *Conjectures* in his old age. A versatile man of letters, he wrote in many literary forms, in terms of the then-current literary conventions. That some of them are no longer in vogue presents difficulties for a modern uninformed reader, but evaluation of his writing requires some knowledge of such conventions so as to read without prejudice and not to reject through ignorance. Even when changes in expectation and taste may interfere with an immediate appeal of certain writings, they may still be of historical significance and interest.

Young does, of course, offer his own barriers to enjoyment in reading. The main one is the undue length of many of his writings —a length often because of prolixity, of repetition of an idea in metaphor after metaphor, resulting in and from a loose organization. Indeed, Young himself was aware of this tendency: "But wherefore such redundancy? such waste of argument?" (*N.* VII, 978–79). His extensive use of the rhetorical devices to which his Oxford training inclined him and his overuse of exclamations and interrogatives tend to seem frequently more artificial than effective. At this point it is well to recall Addison's comment in the *Spectator* (No. 291): "A true critic ought to dwell rather on the Excellencies than Imperfections, to discover the concealed Beauties of a Writer, and communicate to the World such Things as are worth their Observation." Young has indeed many "excellencies" which may still afford pleasure to the reader.

He is frequently extremely effective in extended passages, as in the invocations in the *Night Thoughts* in which the emotional intensity and the lofty expression achieve an anthem-like quality, and in many elaborate and sustained metaphors and similes in which the *Night Thoughts* abound, some of which might stand alone as little poems. But their length forbids illustrative quotation. A shorter metaphoric passage on the transitory nature of life and worldly values shows each detail contributing to the unity of effect:

> For what are men who grasp at praise sublime?
> But bubbles on the rapid stream of time,
> That rise, and fall, that swell, and are no more,
> Born and forgot, ten thousand in an hour? (*Sat.* II)

In striking contrast to his prolixity is his remarkable skill in concise single lines or couplets, conciseness and effectiveness often achieved through metaphor. He writes of imitators of earlier writers: "They meanly live on alms of ages past"; of individual worth apart from status: "It naught avails thee where, but what, thou art," and, in metaphor, "Pygmies are pygmies still, though perch'd on Alps,/And pyramids are pyramids, in vales" (*N.* VI,309–10). Some lines gain their point from connotation, as this one recalling Horace's laboring mountain: "He hems—and is deliver'd of his mouse." Many depend on the pointedness of the satiric implication: "Pursuit of fame with pedants fills our schools"; and, in another example, "And men talk only to conceal the mind."

The pleasure of recognition, plus that of perception of unexpected adaptation, is afforded by Young's delight and skill in giving a surprise twist to familiar expressions: "Which makes a swain as wretched as a king"; "And makes a hell of hell, a heaven of heaven"; "Quadrille has murdered sleep." Another pleasure comes from the many evocative, imaginative lines with suggested imagery: "Chanted beneath the glimpses of the moon" (*N.* IX, 2086); "To drink the spirit of the golden day"; ". . . northern nests of feather'd snow." Because of the long-continued popularity of his writing, many concise lines have become almost like proverbs, well known with no thought of authorship: "Man wants but little, nor that little long" (*N.* IV,118). Probably the most widely known is "Procrastination is the thief of time" (*N.* I,392).

A kind of imperceptible influence has thereby been exerted by Young's poetry. Many lines and passages have been adopted and modified by other writers, perhaps unconsciously; and Young's original authorship is overlooked or unknown. Pope took lines and suggestions from the *Satires*. Gray's lines, "Full many a flower is born to blush unseen,/ And waste its sweetness on the desert air," recall Young's earlier lines from *Job:* "There blooms the rose, where human face ne'er shone,/ And spreads its beauties to the sun alone." Cowper's well-known "man's inhumanity to man" came later than Young's "And endless inhumanities on man" (*N.* VIII,105) and his "And inhumanity is caught from man—/ From smiling man." (*N.* V,158–59). Young's line, "Fantastic chase of shadows hunting shades (*N.* VIII,103) seems to be recalled in Freneau's later lines, "The hunter still the deer pursues,/ The hunter and the deer a shade." Emerson's "Daughters of Time, the hypocritic Days," so different in approaching and after passing by, are much akin to Young's days, "Time's daughters," who deceive all mankind (*N.* VIII,119–30).

Tennyson seems to have many echoes from Young: his lines on the power of prayer, "For so the whole round earth is every way/ Bound by gold chains about the feet of God," are similar to Young's lines on the evidence of the divine seen in the starry skies "Whose love lets down these silver chains of light;/ To draw up man's ambition to himself" (*N.* IX,688–89), and his words in the *Centaur:* "Devotion . . . the golden chain of union between heaven and earth. . . ." The last line in *Resignation,* "Thou alone can'st make our wisdom wise," is recalled in Tennyson's last line of *In Memoriam,* "And in Thy wisdom make me wise." Such echoes from Young appear in many late eighteenth- and nineteenth-century poems and are indicative of his effective expression and of widespread familiarity with his writing.

His greatest writings still have much to offer readers today, as indeed do some of the less great. His keen eye for the absurdities and foibles of mankind and his ability to depict them in telling phrases make the *Satires* delightfully apt today, and one can recognize many contemporaries neatly summed up in his "laughing satire," all the more readable now, as elaborate annotation is, for the most part, not essential for understanding and enjoyment.

Though for many years the *Conjectures* remained forgotten in England, Thomas in his great study of Young called it the "herald of Romanticism" and with Edith Morley's edition, as has been noted, a new interest in it began. Of recent years with the great resurgence of interest in theories of literary criticism, more attention is being given to the *Conjectures,* not so much in separate studies of Young as in books devoted to the whole subject of the Romantic theory of criticism. Of particular interest, M. H. Abrams' most valuable and comprehensive book, *The Mirror and the Lamp,* gives a good deal of consideration to the *Conjectures;* and one can anticipate further studies.

Young's greatest writing is, of course, the *Night Thoughts,* long among the most widely read of poems. Its influence in many aspects of all that is so conveniently labeled "the Romantic movement" was immense. The strain of "romantic melancholy" was not caused by Young's poem, but its development was doubtless influenced by it. But Young's concern with death as a theme, especially in the earlier *Nights,* in line with much writing of the seventeenth and eighteenth century, was part of his interest in reality. People do die. He was primarily concerned with what he considered fundamental reality: the nature of God and man, immortality, the transitory nature of this life and all things of this world. Along with his optimistic belief in the potentialities of human nature, he was "realistic" in his awareness of the actualities of evil, unfortunately in evidence then and now. He was always concerned with the defense of Christianity and enthralled by the new science of Newton as providing new evidence of the divine.

In the twentieth century, though popular interest has sadly faded, various aspects of and topics concerning the *Night Thoughts* have been discussed in scholarly and pseudo-scholarly studies, frequently at quite a remove from Young. There are many questions it would be interesting to explore further: Young's relation, if any, to transcendentalism, for example. But, just as the most interesting of all the *Nights* is the last one, so among the more interesting new approaches to the *Night Thoughts* in contemporary scholarship is that made by Marjorie Nicolson in her studies of the effect of the Newtonian science on men's imagination and poetic expression. In *Mountain Gloom and Mountain Glory: The Development of the Aesthetics of the Infinite,* she devotes some space to an enthusiastic discussion of much of *Night IX;* and she calls Young "space intoxicated" and affected by the "psychology of space." It is in this last *Night* that his growing conception of reality finds its most effective expression in a vision of the infinity of time and space, of a reality that surpasses the grasp of the human mind. Miss Nicolson declares that the keynotes of *Night IX* are greatness and vastness, as they were the basis of his belief, and that in the "nocturnal tour of the heavens" he approaches as closely as human imagination can the "source of Vastness, the true Infinite." She also says that "indeed it was Young who first used the word *progress* with the connotations modern optimism read into it for many years." [2] She is concerned with aspects of his writing and beliefs which invite additional consideration and which afford intellectual pleasure in the reading.

Two hundred years after his death Young is, then, not forgotten with only "the melancholy ghosts of dead renown,/Whisp'ring faint echoes of the world's applause" (*N.* IX,119–20). He still has much of potential value and interest not only for the scholar but also for the general reader. What is needed is greater accessibility of his writings through new editions. More readers might then be able to appreciate Dr. Johnson's concluding comment: "But with all his defects, he was a man of genius and a poet."

Notes and References

Chapter One

1. It is interesting that later YOUNG, the poet, was to be briefly associated with Wharton's son by his second wife and to marry a relative of ANNE WHARTON, the first wife, of the LEE family of Ditchley.

2. PETER SMITHERS, *The Life of Joseph Addison* (Oxford, 1954), considers the Edward Young with Addison to be the poet.

3. A. D. GODLEY, *Oxford in the Eighteenth Century* (New York, 1908), p. 56.

4. *Ibid.*, p. 186.

5. *Ibid.*, p. 205.

6. *Ibid.*, pp. 83–85.

7. ALEXANDER BELJAME, *Men of Letters in the Eighteenth Century 1600–1744* (Paris, 1881), trans. E. O. LORIMER (London, 1948), is the best source of information on the whole subject of patronage.

8. All information on ADDISON and his patrons is derived from SMITHERS, *Life of Joseph Addison.*

9. AARON HILL, *Works* . . . (London, 1753–1754), II, 36.

10. GODLEY, pp. 231–32.

11. RICHARD STEELE, *The Englishman,* ed. RAE BLANCHARD (Oxford, 1955), I, 49–50, Notes, p. 413.

12. BASIL WILLIAMS, *The Whig Supremacy, 1714–1760* (Oxford, 1939), p. 144. An excellent history of the period.

Chapter Two

1. JOSEPH SPENCE, *Anecdotes, Observations, and Characters of Books and Men,* ed. SINGER (London, 1820), p. 147.

2. GEORGE SHERBURN, *The Early Career of Alexander Pope* (Oxford, 1934), pp. 144–45. See also *Correspondence of Alexander Pope* (Oxford, 1956), I, 294.

3. *The Life and Writings of Philip, late Duke of Wharton* (London, 1732), Vol. I. Information about Wharton taken from this volume.

4. SPENCE, p. 351.

5. WALTER THOMAS, *Le Poète Edward Young: Étude sur sa Vie et ses Oeuvres* (Paris, 1901), p. 73.

6. ALLARDYCE NICOLL, *History of English Drama,* Vol. II, 1700–1729 (rev. ed., Cambridge, Eng., 1952–59). Discussion of Augustan tragedy.

7. *The London Stage,* Part 2, 1700–1729, ed. EMMETT L. AVERY (Carbondale, 1960). Introduction, I, xxxix ff.

8. LILY BESS CAMPBELL, "The Rise of the Theory of Stage Presentation during the Eighteenth Century," *Publications of the Modern Language Association of America,* XXXII (1917), 163–200.

9. ASHLEY H. THORNDIKE, *Tragedy* (Boston, 1908), p. 258.

10. See ADDISON, *Spectator,* No. 42, and STEELE, *Tatler,* No. 22.

11. *London Stage, 1700–1729,* I, xix.

12. *Ibid.,* I, c–cii.

13. COLLEY CIBBER, *Apology for his Life* (New York, Everyman ed., n.d.), p. 274.

14. *Ibid.,* p. 94; see also *London Stage, 1700–1729,* I, clvi–clviii.

15. HENRY SHELLEY, *The Life and Letters of Edward Young* (London, 1914), p. 44.

16. DAVID GARRICK, *The Letters of David Garrick,* ed. LITTLE and KAHRL (Cambridge, Mass., 1963), I, 172.

17. JOHN DORAN, *Their Majesties' Servants. Annals of the English Stage* (New York, 1865), I, 261.

18. *Biographia Dramatica,* III, 203.

19. DORAN, I, 276.

20. ARTHUR MURPHY, *The Life of David Garrick, Esq.* (London, 1801), II, 222.

Chapter Three

1. CHALMERS, *English Poets,* XII, 371.

2. SPENCE, p. 374.

3. CHARLOTTE CRAWFORD, "What Was Pope's Debt to Edward Young?" *Journal of English Literary History,* XIII (1946), 157–67.

Chapter Four

1. LADY MARY WORTLEY MONTAGU, *Letters,* ed. Wharncliffe . . . additions by Moy Thomas, 2 v. (New York, 1893), II, 11, 13–14.

2. R. E. TICKELL, *Tickell and the Eighteenth Century Poets, 1685–1740* (London, 1931), p. 105.

3. THOMAS, Appendix B, pp. 582–84.

4. *Ibid.,* pp. 122–23.

5. E. PYLE, *Memoirs of a Royal Chaplain, 1729–1763* (London, 1905), p. 216.

6. *Ibid.,* p. 195.

7. *Ibid.,* p. 160.

8. BENJAMIN LEWIS (LEWIS MELVILLE), *Lady Suffolk and her Circle* (London, 1924), pp. 33, 105, 153, 174, 177.

Chapter Five

1. MRS. DELANY, *The Autobiography and Correspondence* . . . , ed. Lady Llanover (London, 1861), 1st Series, I, 253–54.

2. HENRY PETTIT, "Edward Young and the Case of Lee vs. D'Aranda," *Proceedings of the American Philosophical Society*, CVII (1963), p. 148.

3. SHELLEY, pp. 111–12.

4. THOMAS, Appendix L.

5. H. T. SWEDENBERG, "Letters of Edward Young to Mrs. Judith Reynolds," *Huntington Library Quarterly*, II (1938), 89–100.

6. MRS. DELANY, 1st Series, III, 247.

7. ELIZABETH MONTAGU, *The Queen of the Blue Stockings. Her Correspondence from 1720 to 1761*, ed., Emily J. Climenson (London, 1906), I, 60–61.

8. *Ibid.*, p. 85.

9. *Ibid.*, 90.

10. Letters of EDWARD YOUNG to the Duchess of Portland, 1740–1765, *Calendar of the Manuscripts of the Marquis of Bath*, Vol. I (London, 1904), I, 260–61. Hereafter referred to as *Bath MSS.*

11. MRS. ELIZABETH MONTAGU, I, 204.

12. THOMAS, Appendix H.

13. HENRY PETTIT, *A Bibliography of Young's Night Thoughts* (Boulder, 1954).

Chapter Six

1. PETTIT, *Bibliography* . . . , p. 27, pp. 39–41.

2. H. W. O'CONNOR, "The Narcissa Episode in Young's *Night Thoughts*," *Publications of the Modern Language Association of America*, XXXIV (1919), 130–49.

3. I. ST. J. BLISS, "Thought Background of Young's *Night Thoughts*." (Unpublished Doctoral Dissertation, The University of Chicago, 1931).

4. DEAN EDWARD YOUNG, *Sermons on Several Occasions* (London, 1720), II, 331.

5. I. ST. J. BLISS, "Young's *Night Thoughts* in Relation to Contemporary Christian Apologetics," *Publications of the Modern Language Association of America*, XLIX (1934), 37–70.

Chapter Seven

1. THOMAS, Appendix I, p. 598.

2. GARRICK, I, 172 ff., Letters 108, 117, 121, 122.

3. GEORGE ANNE BELLAMY, *Apology for the Life of George Anne Bellamy* (London, 1786), II, 141.

4. MURPHY, I, 224–31.

5. MARY E. KNAPP, *Prologues and Epilogues of the Eighteenth Century* (New Haven, 1961), "The Metamorphosis of the Comic Epilogue," pp. 286–331.

6. SHELLEY, p. 247.

7. *Bath MSS.*, I, 324.

8. ALAN MCKILLOP, "Richardson Young, and the Conjectures," *Modern Philology*, XXII (1925), 391–404.

9. EDITH MORLEY, ed., EDWARD YOUNG, *Conjectures on Original Composition* (London, 1918), pp. 50–53.

10. JAMES BOSWELL, *Journal of a Tour to the Hebrides*, ed. F. A. POTTLE and C. H. BENNETT (New York, 1936), p. 234.

11. W. R. HUGHES, "Dr. Young and his Curates," *Blackwood's Magazine*, CCXXXI (1932), 623–31. Cf. also *Gentleman's Magazine*, LII, 283–84.

12. SHERBURN, *The Early Career of Alexander Pope* (Oxford, 1934), pp. 5–6.

13. AUSTIN WRIGHT, *Joseph Spence. A Critical Biography* (University of Chicago, 1950), p. 135.

14. THOMAS, Appendix P.

15. *Ibid.*, Appendix Q.

Chapter Eight

1. HUGHES, "Young and his Curates," *Blackwood's Magazine*, CCXXXI (1932), 623–31.

2. MARJORIE NICOLSON, *Mountain Gloom and Mountain Glory* (Ithaca, 1959), pp. 362–67.

Selected Bibliography

PRIMARY SOURCES

YOUNG, EDWARD. *The Works of the Author of the Night Thoughts.* Corrected by himself. A New Edition. 6 vols. London: A. Miller, J. and R. Tonson and others, 1767–1778.

————. *The Complete Works.* Revised and collated with earliest editions. Ed. J. Doran. Preface and annotations by J. Nichols. Biographical introduction by J. Doran. 2 vols. London: William Tegg & Co., 1854.

Letters

One hundred and fifty original Letters between Dr. EDWARD YOUNG and Mr. SAMUEL RICHARDSON. *Monthly Magazine,* December, 1813–August, 1818.

Letters of EDWARD YOUNG to the Duchess of Portland. Calendar of the Manuscripts of the Marquis of Bath. Preserved at Longleat, Wiltshire. Vol. I. *Historical Manuscripts Commission.* London: Printed for His Majesty's Stationery Office, 1904.

Correspondence of Samuel Richardson. Ed. A. L. BARBAULD. 6 vols. London: R. Phillips, 1804. (Many letters to and from YOUNG in Vol. II.)

SECONDARY SOURCES

ABRAMS, M. H. *The Mirror and the Lamp: Romantic Theory and the Critical Tradition.* New York: Oxford University Press, 1953. Valuable study of development of Romantic critical theory with a good deal of consideration of influence of Young.

BAILEY, MARGERY. "Edward Young." *The Age of Johnson.* Essays presented to Chauncey Brewster Tinker. New Haven: Yale University Press, 1949. Good, brief sketch.

BELJAME, ALEXANDRE. *Men of Letters and the English Public in the Eighteenth Century, 1660–1744.* Ed. with introduction by Bonamy Dobrée. Trans. E. O. Lorimer. London: K. Paul, Trench, Truber, 1948. Invaluable study of the patronage system.

BLISS, ISABEL ST. JOHN. "Young's *Night Thoughts* in Relation to Contemporary Christian Apologetics," *Publications of the Modern Language Association of America*, XLIX (1934), 37–70. Study of the extent to which Young followed the arguments of the outstanding defenders of religion of the late seventeenth and early eighteenth century.

CORDASCO, FRANCESCO. *Edward Young: A Handlist of Critical Notices and Studies.* New York: Published for Long Island University Press, by Burt Franklin, 1950. Useful list of miscellaneous studies.

CRAWFORD, CHARLOTTE. "Edward Young and the Wycombe Election," *Modern Language Notes*, LX (1945), 459–61. Supports theory of Young's earlier ordination.

————. "What was Pope's Debt to Edward Young?" *Journal of English Literary History*, XIII (1946), 157–67. Valuable study of evidence of Young's influence on Pope's satires.

DELANY, MRS. MARY GRANVILLE. *The Autobiography and Correspondence of Mary Granville, Mrs. Delany.* Ed. Lady Llanover. London: R. Bentley, Series 1 in 3 vols., 1861; Series 2 in 3 vols., 1862. Of great interest and value in general eighteenth-century background with much comment on Young.

ELLEDGE, SCOTT, ed. *Eighteenth-Century Critical Essays.* 2 vols. Ithaca: Cornell University Press, 1961. Includes Young's "On Lyric Poetry," with discussion and notes in Vol. I. Indication of modern interest in Young's criticism.

GODLEY, A. D. *Oxford in the Eighteenth Century.* London: Methuen & Co., 1908. Useful information about conditions affecting Young's life and style of writing.

HUGHES, W. R. "Dr. Young and his Curates," *Blackwood's Magazine*, CCXXXI (1932), 623–31. Good study, correcting misinformation.

JOHNSON, SAMUEL. *Lives of the Poets.* Ed. G. Birkbeck Hill. Vol. III. Oxford: Clarendon Press, 1905. The "biography" by Croft is the biased source of misinformation. But Johnson's criticism can never be ignored.

MCKILLOP, ALAN D. "Richardson, Young, and the Conjectures," *Modern Philology*, XXII (1925), 391–404. Very valuable study of the influence of Richardson on the revision of the *Conjectures*.

MONTAGU, ELIZABETH. *Elizabeth Montagu: The Queen of the Blue Stockings. Her Correspondence from 1720 to 1761.* Ed. Emily J. Climenson. 2 vols. London: John Murray, 1906. Valuable. Many letters give pictures of Young—episodes, conversation, personality—from 1740 until his death.

MORLEY, EDITH J., ed. *Edward Young's Conjectures on Original Composition.* London: Longmans, Green & Co., 1918. Valuable introduction and information in Bibliography and Appendixes.

NICOLSON, MARJORIE HOPE. *Mountain Gloom and Mountain Glory: The*

Development of the Aesthetics of the Infinite. Ithaca: Cornell University Press, 1959. Contains valuable discussion of Young's "obsession with the psychology of infinity"; suggests a new approach to the interpretation of the *Night Thoughts.*

O'CONNOR, H. W. "The Narcissa Episode in Young's *Night Thoughts,*" *Publications of the Modern Language Association of America,* XXXIV (1919), 130–49. Reviews various versions of the legend.

PETTIT, HENRY. *A Bibliography of Young's "Night Thoughts."* Boulder: Colorado University, 1954. Valuable work with much incidental information.

————. "Edward Young and the Case of Lee vs. D'Aranda," *Proceedings of the American Philosophical Society,* CVII (1963), 145–59. Throws light on Young's close relations with his stepson. Indicates his life less "retired" than has sometimes been thought.

PYLE, EDMUND. *Memoirs of a Royal Chaplain, 1729–1763.* Ed. Albert Hartshorne. London: John Lane, the Bodley Head, 1905. Shows church preferment system from the angle of an opportunist, whose chaplaincy was contemporary with Young's. Illuminating and appalling.

SHELLEY, HENRY C. *The Life and Letters of Edward Young.* London: Sir Isaac Putnam & Sons, 1914. Many letters to Duchess of Portland are included. Effort made to refute Croft. Valuable.

SPENCE, JOSEPH. *Anecdotes, Observations, and Characters of Books and Men.* Ed. Singer. London: W. H. Carpenter, 1820. Contains many anecdotes about Young.

SWEDENBERG, H. T. "Letters of Edward Young to Mrs. Judith Reynolds," *Huntington Library Quarterly,* II (1938), 89–100. Contains letters of 1740–41. Interesting account of Young's brief consideration of a second marriage.

SYKES, REV. NORMAN. *Church and State in England in the Eighteenth Century.* Birkbeck Lectures. Trinity College, Cambridge, 1931–32. Hamden, Conn.: Archon Books, 1962. Good account of the whole system of church preferment and appointments.

THOMAS, WALTER. *Le Poète Edward Young: Étude sur sa Vie et ses Oeuvres.* Paris: Hachette et Cie, 1901. Indispensable. Most thorough and extensive study of Young and his works. The numerous appendixes contain valuable material and letters otherwise inaccessible. Since written, some details need to be modified as Young's letters and other material have become available.

TICKELL, RICHARD EUSTACE. *Thomas Tickell and the Eighteenth Century Poets (1685–1740). Containing Numerous Letters and Poems Hitherto Unpublished.* London: Constable & Co., 1931. Contains nineteen letters from Young, before 1730. Establishes date of his ordination.

TILLOTSON, GEOFFREY. "Eighteenth Century Poetic Diction." *Eighteenth Century English Literature. Modern Essays in Criticism.* Ed. James L. Clifford. New York: Oxford University Press, 1959. Valuable account of some poetic conventions influencing Young and his contemporaries.

Index